OUT

Social Sculpture
2001
Roll of beige contract carpeting, 25 x 25 x 207cm
Installation view at John Hansard Gallery

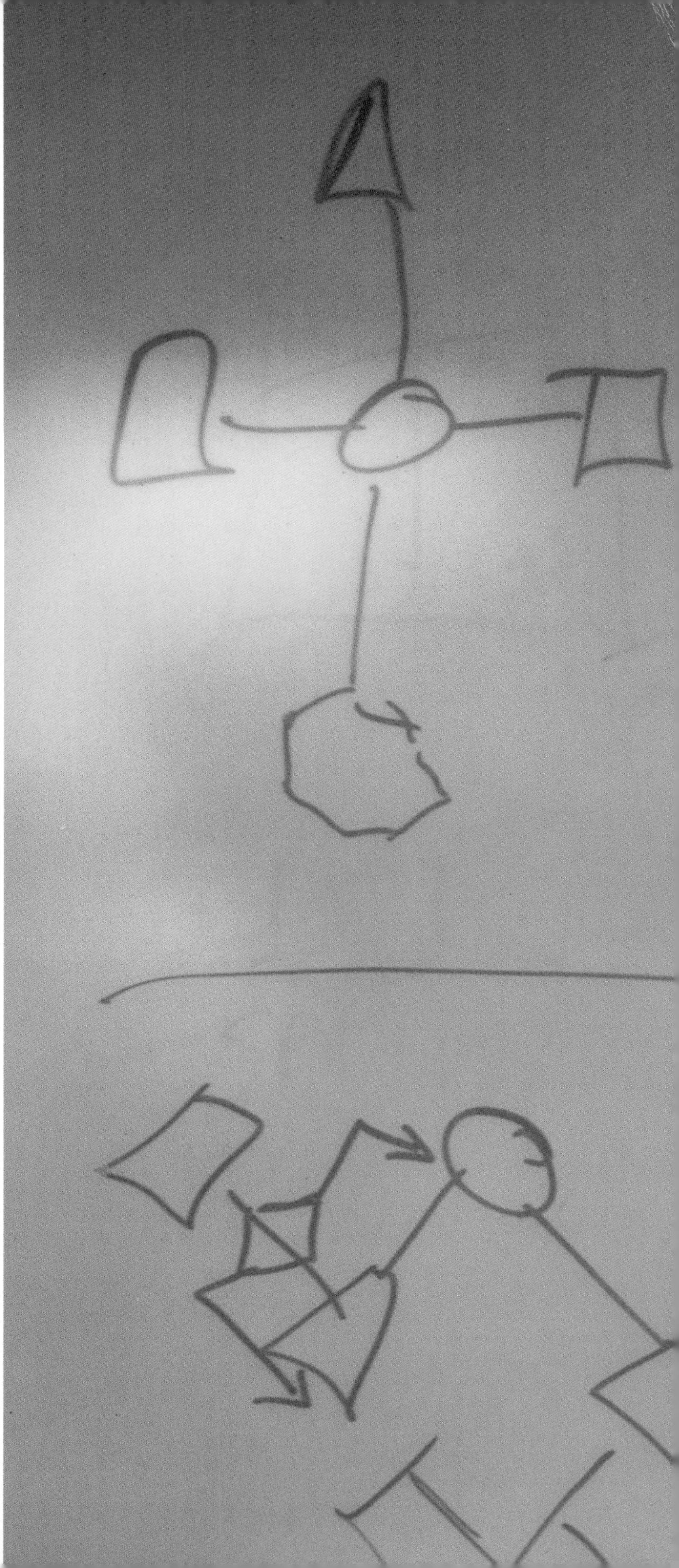

Meta Patterns

Architecture of Business

Artistically Abstract

Introduction
Steven Bode

In early November 1999, Carey Young and I were photographed in the Film and Video Umbrella offices holding up a cheque that I had signed and was about to present to her. This slightly self-conscious 'photo-opportunity' was intended to inaugurate an ongoing twelve-month project in which Young would invest her £1,000 commission fee in a portfolio of shares on the internet. The fluctuating fortunes of the two separate sets of investments – one in a range of new-technology companies listed under the banner of 'Art', the other grouped under the heading of 'Life' – would form the basis of the work, with changes in the 'value' of these two great existential imperatives to be charted on a dedicated web page. Young invested the money with a broker, and updates (in the form of flow charts and other graphical information) were posted to the site at regular intervals. Almost exactly twelve months later, an investment company with the uncannily appropriate name of Artist Acquisition stepped in to enquire if she wanted to sell her shares, bringing this ephemeral conceptual experiment to a supernaturally tidy conclusion — and making Young a tidy profit into the bargain. Although she didn't offer to cut us in on any of her margin, I was secretly very impressed. As well the ability to generate some very nice graphs, Carey Young clearly had something of a flair for business.

In the intervening years, Young's stock as an artist has continued to rise, even as the shares in those technology companies (or at least those that remain in existence) have plummeted in price. During that time, Young has steadily accumulated an incisive and arresting body of work which, while continuing to draw upon ideas and methodologies from the forefront of the network economy, has extended its aim to encompass a wider field of corporate identity and iconography. Many of the works in her first solo touring exhibition, 'Business as Usual' (curated by Film and Video Umbrella, and first staged in collaboration with John Hansard Gallery, Southampton), revolve around subtle, often deadpan, interventions within a range of corporate environments. The resulting works (documented on video, in photographs or over a number of wall-based texts) play, in deft and disarming ways, with the language of leading-edge business — parodying its penchant for neologisms and jargon while, at the same time, testing its claims as one of the few remaining repositories of radically new and innovative thinking.

'Carey Young, Incorporated' is the first survey publication devoted to her work, and the ideas and influences that inform it. Featuring four newly-written texts (including one co-authored by the artist herself), it explores the intellectual and cultural backdrop to this new metaphysics of business, evaluating its pretensions to modernity against a paradigm of creativity and innovation that has become enshrined within the contemporary art world. As well as showcasing the newly-commissioned works created for 'Business as Usual', the book highlights a number of equally provocative pieces produced before, or in parallel to, that exhibition. Ever since our first collaboration in 1999, Carey Young has continued to present Film and Video Umbrella (and, by extension, her audience) with a series of intriguing and occasionally disconcerting conceptual challenges. But for our part, at least, these proposals (and the leaps of the imagination they entail) have had the habit of developing into some of the most stimulating and satisfying projects we have made. Three years on, I think it would be safe to say that Carey Young has more than repaid our initial investment.

Steven Bode, Film and Video Umbrella, London, March 2002

NatWest   60-40-04

7

Chancery Lane and Holborn Branch
PO Box No159, 332 High Holborn, London WC1V 7PS

Date _4/11/99_

Pay _CAREY YOUNG_

ONE THOUSAND POUNDS   £1000-00

ONLY

National Westminster Bank Plc   FOR & BEHALF OF FILM & VIDEO
201201   UMBRELLA LIMITED

Account Payee

Cheque No.   Branch Sort Code   Account No.

⑆002583⑆ 60⑇4004⑈ 46097549⑈02

October 1, 1999

To Whom It May Concern
re: Carey Young

This is to confirm that Film and Video Umbrella have
commissioned the above named person to produce an
artwork as part of the exhibition entitled the.year.dot.

As part of the production of this artwork, Carey Young
will invest not more than £1000 of the commissioning fee
awarded to her by Film and Video Umbrella.

Permission to use the fee in this manner has been
granted by Film and Video Umbrella and the funders of
this project.

The intentions of the artist in this regard are fully
recognised and understood by Film and Video Umbrella.

It is anticipated that the artist may request permission
for the recording by means of photography or video of
transactions that will take place in the process of
investing this money.

Your assistance in the realisation of any such requests
would be very much appreciated.

If you have questions or need for clarification, please do
not hesitate to contact me.

Yours faithfully,

Steven Bode
Director, Film and Video Umbrella

To: "'carey young'"
From: "'Michael Thomson'"
Subject: Purchase of American Shares
Date: Wed, 5 Jan 2000 19:47:24 -0000

Dear Ms Young,

I am writing to confirm that we have
purchased the following stocks for you
from the US Market:

31 shares in ART
(AC Neilsen Corporation) @ £14.75
48 shares in LIFE
(Lifeline Systems Inc) @ £9.75

The Exchange Rate at the time of your
deals was £=US$1.6424

I will send you the actual Advice Notes
for the above trades to you tomorrow via
email, however in the meantime if you have
any other questions or queries please
don't hesitate to contact us.

Yours,

MICHAEL THOMSON
Fastrade

FASTRADE ADVICE NOTE

TORRIE & CO
132 ROSE STREET
EDINBURGH
EH2 3JD
Tel: 0131 467 8464
Fax: 0131 220 2363
E-MAIL: stockbrokers@torrie.co.uk

DATE: 05/01/A0

MS C YOUNG

We have today, subject to the Rules
and Regulations of The London Stock
Exchange and The Securities & Futures
Authority Ltd

BOUGHT   31 ART

AC NEILSON CORP COM STK
US$0.01
@ 1475
QUANTITY   31
PRICE (Pence)   1475
BGN CONDS
CONSIDERATION   GBP457.25

COMMISSION   GBP30.00

==
NET TOTAL   GBP487.25

==

BARGAIN REF: B71427DEP
TIME: 1553
BROKER: 905
SETTLEMENT DUE DATE: 10/01/A0 "U"
In view of Capital Gains Tax it is
essential that all Contract notes and
Statements should be retained by
clients
(E.&.O.E.)

==
==

FASTRADE ADVICE NOTE

TORRIE & CO
132 ROSE STREET
EDINBURGH
EH2 3JD
Tel: 0131 467 8464
Fax: 0131 220 2363
E-MAIL: stockbrokers@torrie.co.uk

DATE: 05/01/A0

MS C S R YOUNG

We have today, subject to the Rules
and Regulations of The London Stock
Exchange and The Securities & Futures
Authority Ltd

BOUGHT   48 LIFE

LIFELINE SYSTEMS INC COM STK
US$0.02
@ 975
QUANTIT   48
PRICE (Pence)   975
BGN CONDS
CONSIDERATION   GBP468.00

COMMISSION   GBP30.00

==
NET TOTAL   GBP498.00

==

BARGAIN REF: B71428DEP
TIME: 1649
BROKER: 905
SETTLEMENT DUE DATE: 10/01/A0 "U"
In view of Capital Gains Tax it is
essential that all Contract notes and
Statements should be retained by
clients
(E.&.O.E.)

==
==

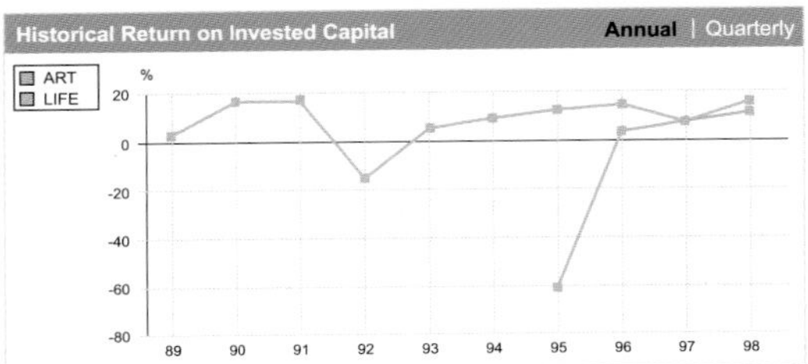

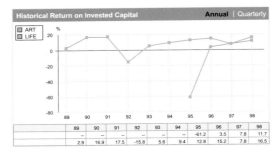

	89	90	91	92	93	94	95	96	97	98
	--	--	--	--	--	--	-61.2	3.5	7.8	11.7
	2.9	16.9	17.5	-15.8	5.6	9.4	12.8	15.2	7.8	16.5

Typical annual return on an investment in ART and LIFE
(source: www.quicken.com)

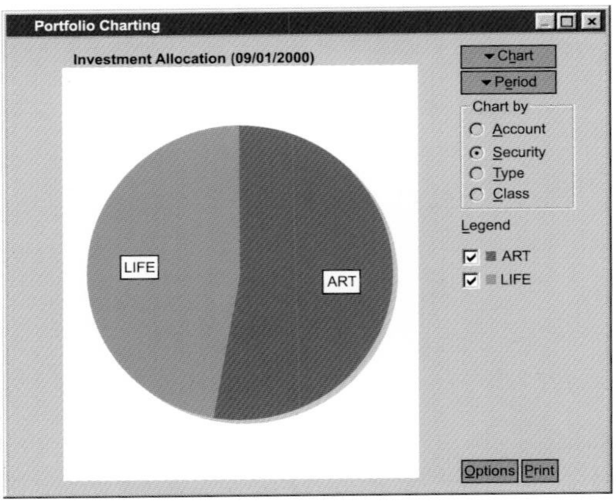

Typical annual return on an investment in ART and LIFE
(source: www.quicken.com)

Historical Comparison	1 Year (TTM)	3 Years	5 Years	10 Years
	Company	Industry	Ranking*	
ART Revenue	7.45%	14.17%		
LIFE Revenue	10.75%	20.01%		
ART Net Income	39.34%	-82.77%		
LIFE Net Income	41.38%	78.93%		
ART Cash Flow	12.36%	-30.53%		
LIFE Cash Flow	32.86%	86.38%		

* Company vs Industry ranking: weaker stronger

Historical comparison of ART and LIFE
(source: www.quicken.com)

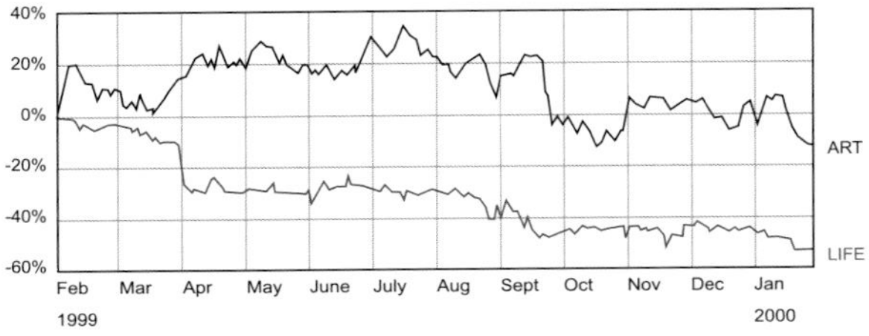

ART and LIFE performance comparison (updated every month)
(source: www.quicken.com)

Art and Life
1999 – 2000
Web site
£1,000 cheque, introductory letter from project funder, text derived from email conversations, web-based stock portfolio graphing tools from a variety of financial information web sites, financial data from international stockmarkets.

A commission fee of one thousand pounds, made to the artist by Film and Video Umbrella, was invested in two corporations, AC Nielsen and Lifeline Systems, Inc., traded on the NYSE and NASDAQ stock exchanges under the acronyms 'ART' and 'LIFE'. The site showed documentation of the artist's working process and portrayed the fate of these investments as they competed against each other on the international money markets, via graphs and charts derived from web-based stock analysis software tools. The project was ended almost exactly one year later, by a corporate takeover of the company 'ART' by the VNU N.V. Corporation, via a holding company named 'Artist Acquisition's, at which point the artist sold her shares in both ART and LIFE.

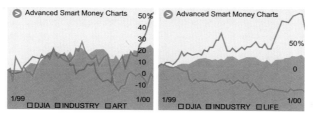

ART and LIFE compared to Industry and Dow Jones Industrial Average
(source: www.smartmoney.com)

Rating by Our Community -- Rate ART!

Rating	**Strong buy**
Last Trade	24
Target Price	35
Number of ratings	4

Top Community Ratings — Updated 2:44PM PT, Jan 9

Rating by Our Community -- Rate LIFE!

Rating	**Buy**
Last Trade	14
Target Price	23.50
Number of ratings	2

Top Community Ratings — Updated 2:45PM PT, Jan 9

Community ratings for ART and LIFE
(source: www.quicken.com)

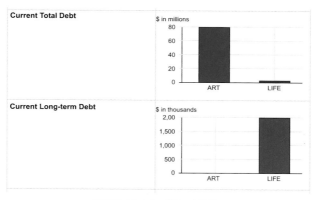

Current debts for ART and LIFE
(source: www.quicken.com)

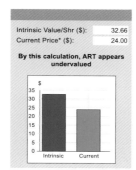
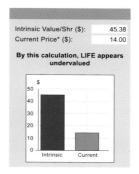

Intrinsic Value/Shr ($):	32.66
Current Price* ($):	24.00

By this calculation, ART appears undervalued

Intrinsic Value/Shr ($):	45.38
Current Price* ($):	14.00

By this calculation, LIFE appears undervalued

Comparison of ART and LIFE according to intrinsic value
(source: www.quicken.com)

The Avant Garde, Again
Alex Farquharson

So what will be required in the future? Answer: 'sole creators... defined by ideas', 'disruptive innovation', and 'a shift from... tangibles to intangibles'. These phrases aren't lifted from an award ceremony speech by the curator of an international Biennale, but from an article in 'Fast Company', a leading business magazine. [1] "Where is the Next Frontier of innovation?" we're told is the question we should continually be asking ourselves. "The only way... today," the unnamed author concludes, "is to be fully, constantly, and instantly alive — alive to new ideas, alive to new practices, alive to new opportunities." Never before have the lexicons of contemporary art and leading-edge business, with their mutual emphases on discovery, creativity, and innovation, sounded so alike.

Opinions are sharply divided on whether the infamous 2000 crash of technology stocks was a period of adjustment of the kind that inevitably accompanies any radical change, or a return to traditional 'common sense' business values (the unnamed 'Fast Company' reporter is obviously of the former opinion). Either way, the theme of constant innovation has long been a core tenet of both capitalist economies and Twentieth century art. Corporations consistently evoke the concept of innovation to link their values with those of artists, even in instances where artists believe their innovations are hostile to the corporate ethos. Way back in 1969, the tobacco giant, Philip Morris, outlining its reasons for sponsoring the seminal Conceptual/post-Minimal exhibition 'When Attitudes Become Form' (curated by Harald Szeemann and shown at Kunsthalle, Berne and ICA, London) wrote, in the exhibition catalogue:

"Just as the artist endeavours to improve his interpretation and conceptions through innovation, the commercial entity strives to improve its end-product or service through experimentation with new methods and materials. Our constant search for a new and better way in which to perform and produce is akin to the questionings of artists whose works are represented here." [2]

Philip Morris' act of identifying the avant-garde's strategies with its own would have been a particularly bitter irony to swallow in this instance, since these were types of art practice predicated on the belief that physical dissolution was, at least in part, driven by the will to evade commodification. Thus, for theorist Lucy Lippard, the 'de-materialisation' of the art object into ideas, gestures and processes was a bid by artists to act outside capitalism. In the same year as the Philip Morris/'Attitudes' joint-venture, Lippard stated "The artists who are trying to do non-object art are introducing a drastic solution to the problem of artists being bought and sold so easily, along with their art" in an interview that became the Preface to 'Six Years', her survey of these art tendencies eventually published in 1973. By the time she wrote the Postface to 'Six Years' in 1972, that idealism had faded altogether:

"It seemed in 1969... that no one, not even a public greedy for novelty, would actually pay money, or much of it, for a xerox sheet referring to an event [etc]... it seemed that these artists would therefore be forcibly freed from the tyranny of a commodity status and market-orientation. Three years later, the major conceptualists are selling work for substantial sums here and in Europe; they are represented by... the world's most prestigious galleries. Clearly whatever minor revolutions in communication have been achieved by the process of de-materialising the object... art and artist in a capitalist society remain luxuries." [3]

Hans Haacke had foreseen this outcome. Earlier he'd been making post-Minimalist 'de-materialised' works whose forms were the results of physical systems or processes — air flows, water flows and condensation patterns produced by pumps and fans, for example. Dependent for their form on a mechanical source of energy, the space around them, and the passage of time, Haacke's early 'sculptures' were physical states rather than static, autonomous objects. When he moved his attention to the spaces that framed these works, it wasn't just static, white, minimalist boxes he saw, but systems, processes, connections and flows, much as before, only this time of a political and economic kind. For Haacke, the prevalent notion of 'site' was merely an institutional membrane connecting art's avant-garde to global corporate and political networks, via the cultural brokerage of exhibition sponsorship and museum board membership. Harald Szeemann's 'Attitudes' were Philip Morris' too.

If there was a paradigm for the disparate avant-garde art forms of the late 60s and early 70s it was the endeavour to draw what had been the mutually exclusive realms of 'Art' and 'Life' much closer together; to break out of the physical, social and ideological confines of the museum and merge the avant-garde with the progressive politics and the everyday social flow of the contemporaneous counter-culture.

It didn't quite turn out like that. Fast forward to the new century, and it's clear that very few aspects of our lives on the one hand, or strategies of avant-garde subversion on the other, haven't been appropriated by global brands and marketed back to us. Very few aspects of society, including our cultural institutions, are truly public anymore — most are sponsored by, partnered with or outsourced to for-profit businesses.

~

Carey Young, dressed in a smart business suit, paces back and forth in a slick office space. The wall behind her is made entirely of glass. It looks out onto the vast central atrium of a sparkling post-modern office complex. Beyond the atrium are similar offices to the one she's in, where executives in shirt-sleeves sit before computer monitors. Young is alone in the room with a tall middle-aged man, also smartly dressed, who is in the process of offering her instruction — coaxing her, giving praise and supporting her efforts with constructive advice. "I am a revolutionary," Young exclaims for the n'th time, weary but determined to better her delivery. Again, but with different emphasis: "I... am a revolutionary." She doesn't sound quite certain, and knows she needs to believe what she's saying herself if she is to convince the prospective audience. Alisdair Chisholm of Marcus Bohn Associates, a company that specialises in business skills training, sketches out a scenario, and, improvising, alludes to passages of the speech we haven't heard that are supposed to have preceded this declaration. He encourages her to step a couple of paces towards her audience on reaching the tricky phrase; towards us, in fact, since, when the work is projected, the room appears life-size, and we seem to occupy the other half of the office space that the screen seems to bisect.

Carey Young's 'I am a Revolutionary' is, on one level, a delirious post-modern reading of Keith Arnatt's Wittgensteinian 'Trouser Word Piece' (1972) — a photo of the artist holding a sign that reads 'I AM A REAL ARTIST'. Young's video performance includes Arnatt's original tautologies while overlaying them with contemporary corporate versions of each term: artist/businesswoman rehearses artistic statement/corporate speech about herself in an art video/corporate training video for a small art audience/imaginary business audience. As well as Arnatt's work, the substitution of 'revolutionary' for 'artist' evokes Joseph Beuys, implying that today's corporate guru is the progeny of Beuys' now antiquated radical shaman routine; his legendary persuasive powers and inexhaustible ego now re-directed from participatory democracy to profit. But why are these four words causing her so much trouble? Is it, as artist, because she can't quite bring herself to believe in either the avant-garde or political utopia, if that is her message? Or, as executive, does she doubt that she is indeed a radical leader, a visionary? Or, can't she bring herself to accept the co-option of the rhetoric of radical politics by modern-day business, and the redundancy of opposition that that seems to imply?

Joseph Beuys' own take on the art/life dichotomy was that the active re-shaping of society by the people themselves was itself a form of art — an art he termed 'social sculpture'. His primary medium for propagating this idea was a didactic form of performance in which the use of language and speech was instrumental — "to be a teacher is my greatest work of art," he said. [4] For the entire duration of Documenta V (1972), he put himself in the position of the art work in what he called an 'office', rather than 'gallery', where people could meet with him at all times for social and political debate ('One Hundred Days of the Information Office of the Organisation for Direct Democracy through Referendum'). Carey Young's recent 'corporate works' re-locate Beuys' notion of social sculpture within the modern business environment; its 'soft' yet didactic techniques of training, brainstorming and skills workshops displacing Beuys' charismatic proselytising and, with it, by implication, his utopian vision for society. In an act of double irony, Beuys' parodic 'Office' becomes, quite simply, an office. Another work, 'Social Sculpture' (2001), performs a similar manoeuvre, whereby Beuys' famous rolls of felt – that in his symbolic world signified the preservation of human life – are substituted by a roll of its visual equivalent in the modern workplace: beige contract carpeting.

In 'Everything You've Heard is Wrong' (1999), Young herself assumes the role of the instructor, this time at Speakers' Corner in Hyde Park (a piece that 'I am a Revolutionary,' in many ways, mirrors and reverses). Speakers' Corner is itself a kind of cacophonic mini-Beuysian participatory democracy, where anyone, no matter what their status, can get up on a 'soapbox' – actually, a stepladder – and promote their world-view to whoever happens to be assembled. Providing a forum for the amateur orator, the fanatic, the oddball or the disenfranchised, it is inevitably a site for more left-field or idiosyncratic opinion. In the video of the performance, Young is shown giving a sober 'skills workshop' on corporate presentation, again dressed impeccably in a businesswoman's suit. On an obvious level the humour derives from the disparity between the methodologies Young advocates and the calmness of her delivery, compared to the style and content (religious, political, other) of her neighbours' more feverish oratory. Though the corporate persona Young adopts believes her act to be a helpful one, and that her audience shares her aspirations, the dark lining of the humour resides in the unwelcome proposition that even this carnival of free-thought might be absorbed by the corporate world some time in the not-so-distant future. The title 'Everything You've Heard is Wrong', which is borrowed from the title of a business book, suggests further paradoxes and ambivalences: does it mean to say that it's the 'presentation skills' of her fellow speakers that's at fault (i.e. on the level of the signifier), or that their messages are 'wrong' too (the signified)? More generally, is it suggesting that all the knowledge we've each acquired throughout our lives is now corrupted? Or self-reflexively, is it saying that it's what the piece itself appears to represent – i.e. the corporate absorption of free debate – that's 'wrong'? Characteristically, Young presents us with continuum rather than closure.

For 'Incubator' (2001), Young 'outsourced' this role to Pól Ó Móráin: a venture capitalist with Xerox Venture Labs, where the artist was undertaking a residency funded by East England Arts. Small start-up companies formed within Xerox as a result of their research work go through an 'incubation' period, nurtured by teams of specialists, before they are let loose in the wilds of the market. A vital component of this process is brainstorming, here called a 'visioning workshop,' where the directors of infant companies are encouraged to think radically, and perhaps abstractly, about the potential for their business — to come up with 'crazy ideas' and 'blue sky scenarios', irrespective of their current resources. These are then compared with examples from a wide range of industry sectors in order to help breed the Darwinian fittest.

The participants in the visioning workshop in 'Incubator' were the directors of Anthony Wilkinson Gallery, the small-ish, respected commercial space in East London. After the event, the work existed as an edited video of the two-hour workshop, the office furniture and detritus of the meeting, along with the full transcript of the proceedings, together with Ó Móráin's follow-up suggestions in preparation for subsequent sessions, reproduced on a Xerox copier, of course, and available for sale as an inexpensive multiple (the artist ironically returning to traditional modes of selling works of art).

The workshop began by focusing on defining the gallery's product and its existing markets. Despite the innovation and diversity of contemporary art itself, from Pól Ó Móráin's business perspective, the way it is sold is conventional, outmoded and unimaginative. This first half of the workshop confirmed his impressions: product (art) from the same dozen or so suppliers (artists) is shown in one outlet (the gallery), and marketed conventionally through ads in trade (art) magazines to three market segments (private collectors, museums and corporate collections).

The gallery directors were then encouraged to identify new market segments, new ways of reaching them, ways of increasing product supply, or not seeing what they're offering as a product at all, but as a service or an experience along the lines of the ways most products are now marketed to consumers (as aspirational lifestyle, for example). This way of thinking necessarily involves breaking the mould of the gallery system. It also rides roughshod over the principle that it is the artists' role to determine the art they make, as one of Ó Móráin's lines of enquiry makes clear:

"How do you define the lifetime of an artist?"... "Don't you try to influence what the artists produce?"... "Do you think there is any flexibility in terms of generating more pieces of art per artist?"... "But if you take that piece of art and produce it in a hundred different colours then isn't that still unique?"... "What we're trying to do here is not necessarily what's right. In other words, could you have an exploitative approach to art and art marketing?"

The gallery directors respond in three different ways: either by following his lead with suggestions of their own, or not responding at all, or by hitting the brakes — a representative example of the latter is: "Well, I think in the end a gallery is a gallery. It's about a space that puts on exhibitions. You can't really get away from that." Ó Móráin responds by laying down some basic market principles: "There's a concept in the marketplace in general that you don't in any sense expect the client to come to you. You understand who they are, where they are, and what they want, and you bring the product to them. You give it to them in any way that makes it easy for them."

By discounting 'what's right' (the interests of the gallery's artists, the creative
integrity of the art work, the idea that art cannot be reduced to commodity, the
reluctance to be seen to be commercially motivated, etcetera), the objective becomes
very pure — to increase profit. By cutting out the ethical paradoxes that inevitably
enfold the business of art, the venture capitalist is able to conceive of radical ways of
expanding art's market and perhaps its potential audience (art investment portfolios,
product placement in celebrities' houses, exhibitions at professional networking
events, television ads, hospitality on Concorde, and so on).

Ironically, many of Ó Móráin's examples reflect key innovations of the avant-garde
of the last century, such as the multiple, intervention, art-as-commerce, the site-
specific, the notion that the avant-garde is perpetually renewing itself (built-in
obsolescence), the artist as service provider, and the idea that the artist may
outsource the actual making of objects. Young, in fact, has incorporated most of
these avant-garde strategies in the form of 'Incubator' itself, along with specific
references to two 70s works that broke the art/money taboo early on: Chris Burden's
'Full Financial Disclosure' (1977), a disclosure of his year's earnings on television,
and Michael Asher's untitled act of removing the wall dividing the exhibition space
and the office at Copley Gallery, in L.A. in 1974. In 'Incubator' the vectors of the
avant-gardes of art and the information economy converge uncannily — what were
binary oppositions appear entwined, rhizomatically, in a single matrix. Ironically it's
the business structure around art that clings to the conventional 'value propositions'
(Ó Móráin) of its product and market: scarcity, uniqueness, permanence; exclusivity,
prior knowledge, single outlets, existing markets. When it comes to the business of
art, it seems artists have a monopoly on innovation. 'Incubator' appears to draw the
ironic conclusion that avant-garde artists have more in common with leading-edge
business strategists than with gallerists that sell their work.

In 'Nothing Ventured', shown at fig-1 in London and Northern Gallery of
Contemporary Art in Sunderland, Carey Young again constructed a 'social
sculpture', and a notion of the artist, from corporate language and interfaces.
Physically, the piece consisted of just a telephone on a table with a single chair.
Thus far it was reminiscent of Walter de Maria's 'Art by Telephone', exhibited in
'When Attitudes Become Form', though he didn't stretch to providing the furniture.
By de Maria's phone was a sign that read: "If this telephone rings, you may answer
it. Walter de Maria is on the line and would like to talk to you." This was the voice
of the artist as voice of God — mysterious, immanent, invisible, omnipresent.
(As it happened, God never called). In 'Nothing Ventured' it wasn't the artist on the
other line, but one of around thirty call centre agents the artist had employed for
the duration of the show. On lifting the receiver, a call would go through to one of
these agents who would attempt to categorise the caller as "a member of the press,
a prospective customer or a general enquiry." The caller then had to choose from a
menu of four options: "biographical information, previous exhibitions, themes
and influences, or reviews and review quotes." If the caller selected a quote, the
operator read out one from 'Mute' magazine: "Young's work retains a ludic
approach that should not be written off as co-opted." Influences, callers were told,
include "the artist Joseph Beuys and his notion of social sculpture, i.e. that everyone
can create art."

The situation set up a tension between the information providers, who presumably
knew little about art concepts other than what was in the script, and the receiver,
who tended to know a lot more about the context of the work, and who felt their
privilege and freedom undermined. Consequently, as gathered by Young in the
documentation of the calls, many visitors attempted to interrupt the script, and
reverse the lines of authority, by asking the operator to elaborate on what they

meant by the artist wanting to break down "the barriers between commerce and art," for instance. At this point the agent would have to improvise by recourse to his or her own opinions, thus rupturing the generic facade.

A related piece by Young is a readymade in the form of a white board, retrieved from a call centre, listing a number of 'Gap Fillers' — phrases all of us would recognise as techniques agents use to buy time and fill silence, e.g. "I am just awaiting confirmation..." or "I am searching for your details, please bear with me..." Today's service sector no longer presents itself as mechanical, impersonal and bureaucratic — the *bear with me's* and *just's* we're getting accustomed to hearing suggest an informal 'one-to-one' empathy and intimacy between employee and customer, though this air of spontaneity is carefully regulated through training, scripts and recorded conversations. The benign language of 'customer care' instils in us a sense of identification with a product or service, through identification with individual employees. The title of Carey Young's exhibition at Oxford Street's Virgin Megastore – simply 'My Megastore' – evoked this process of brand identification, while alluding to the various discrete counter-strategies Young put in place to expose the behind-the-scenes mechanism of big-brand customer relations ('Always Smile at the Customer', lifted from Virgin's training manual, was programmed into the LCD displays of the Megastore's tills, for example).

In 'Nothing Ventured' Carey Young turned herself into a product, on par with all the other commercial offerings her call centre agents were spending the rest of their time promoting. Callers could, if they wanted to, acquire a fair bit of information about the artist and her work. Yet, by outsourcing the P.R. role to a call centre rather than a gallery, she was, in effect, outsourcing her artistic identity to a corporate framework. In 'Nothing Ventured' the 'real' Carey Young was no more present than the Walter de Maria who never called. "Good afternoon, Carey Young, 'Nothing Ventured'," the agents greeted each caller, a picture of the individual so exteriorised that it is adopted with ease by any number of others. 'Carey Young' in 'Nothing Ventured' draws a parallel between post-modern 'death of the author' strategies, such as Cindy Sherman's adoption of multiplicitous Hollywood female stock types in the 'Untitled Film Stills', and the way employees of a corporation, especially one called after the proper name of its founder, adopt its brand identity. 'Nothing Ventured' also could be seen as a comment on the recent phenomenon of galleries and museums outsourcing their P.R. to specialist firms. Art critics and editors are now cold-called by people who know a script but not the subject.

The double-irony in 'Nothing Ventured' was that Young, on a simple, pragmatic level, was playfully maximising the promotional possibilities of her first solo show (perhaps also parodying the reputation 'young British artists' have for self-promotion). The title evoked this by punning on the old saying, 'nothing ventured, nothing gained' (Young cheekily admitting she's got a nerve), and, of course, the inherent association with 'venture capital'. At the end each caller was given the option of receiving more information by post and to be entered on Young's database for invitations to subsequent exhibitions, an offer that deliberately evoked junk mail.

By presenting herself as a brand and her art as a product, Young appears to jettison art's transcendent values, opening up her practice to the vulgar, unsentimental vagaries of the open market. In an earlier piece, 'Art and Life', she did just that by investing a £1,000 public art commission grant in two stocks, one with the ticker symbol 'ART', the other with the ticker symbol 'LIFE'. The piece ended a year later when Young's shares in 'ART', which was out-performing 'LIFE', was acquired by a corporation named, spookily enough, 'Artist Acquisition' (thus giving her a reasonable profit on her initial investment). "To my knowledge this is the world's first art project to be ended by corporate take-over," Young reflected.

In a new video, 'Getting to Yes', Young, dressed for business, stands at a lectern in an empty corporate auditorium, its rather sublime blue interior reminiscent of works by James Turrell or Yves Klein. As in 'I am a Revolutionary', she is rehearsing a speech for an implied audience, but this time it is an acceptance speech. The three short paragraphs narrate a kind of corporate take-over of the artist, though given that the persona Young adopts mentions her paintings, and Young does not paint, we can conclude she may not be referring to herself. From the time the artist's works are bought for the corporate collection, this artist gradually finds herself relinquishing her autonomy to the flattering and apparently benign advances of a 'mighty' corporation. First she agrees to a sponsored party at her opening, then allows her images to be used in a company report, then runs a "creative thinking workshop" for some of their "top people," until eventually her sense of self as an artist dissolves altogether and she gratefully accepts a position in this "mighty" corporation: "And of course, I said yes! To all of those things"; "I shall devote myself entirely to achieving your objectives."

The narrative trajectory of the video is a kind of travesty of Carey Young's own increased involvement in business, both in art and life. Her first job at a major IT and management consultancy was to give occasional presentations on uses of new technology to corporate clients — the company had a policy of deliberately selecting 'creatives' for this task. Young still distinctly recalls, with a sense of self-estrangement, the time she first identified her employer's interests as her own by saying the word 'we' instead of 'me/them'. 'Getting to Yes' includes the gallery audience in the equation, by appearing to position us amongst the auditorium's rows of empty chairs, since they form the foreground of the projected image. By implication we may also be on the 'slippery-slope' to a corporate take-over. It's an impression that's unmistakably uncanny: her contamination of 'business' with the virus 'art', and, at the same time, 'art' with the virus 'business', is, indeed, a little dislocating, perhaps alienating, but whatever shuddering this cross-contamination may induce is rapidly replaced by laughter when we begin to unravel the layered ironies that go into their conception. The *doppelgängers* she makes of avant-garde art and leading-edge business may appear indistinguishable, but for the time being, at least, they remain, for the most part, separate, if parallel worlds.

Alex Farquharson

Footnotes

1   'What is the State of the New Economy?', 'Fast Company' Magazine, September 2001
2   Sponsor's Statement for 'When Attitudes Become Form', John A. Murphy, in 'Art in Theory' ed. Charles Harrison & Paul Wood, (Blackwell 1993) p886
3   'Six Years', Lucy Lippard, extract in 'Art in Theory' ed. Charles Harrison & Paul Wood, (Blackwell 1993) p895
4   'Conceptual Art', Tony Godfrey, (Phaidon 1998) p195

① MY NAME...

PRES. SKILLS
SPEAKER'T CORNER.

• HOBBY

• BUSINESS

• IMPROVE CONFIDENCE ╱ SHY
                      ╲ SELF CONSCIOUS

CONVINCE + PEOPLE - IDEAS.
INSPIRE
• I BELIEVE EVERYONE —— LEARN - SPEAK

... SOMETHING USEFUL.
• WHAT? egs..

above
Everything You've Heard is Wrong
1999
Production still from video of performance by the artist
at Speakers' Corner, London
Video: 6.35 minutes; colour, sound

opposite
Everything You've Heard is Wrong
Prompt cards

I am a Revolutionary
2001
Production still
Video: 4.08 minutes; colour, sound

With thanks to Alisdair Chisholm of Marcus Bohn Associates, the business skills training company.

Getting to Yes
2001
Video: 4.22 minutes; colour, sound
Installation view at John Hansard Gallery
with thanks to Bloomberg

Adventures in Capitalism
John Kelsey

While art has no monopoly on creativity, it remains our 'change agent' *par excellence*, prized less for the objects or images it produces than for the flexibility of its processes, its playfulness, and its capacity to conjure up difference where everything is the same. But what if art chose to stop being different, or attempted to experience sameness in a different way? This is how we start to imagine an art that negotiates away the last traces of its otherness in order to become imperceptible and integrate itself all the more insidiously into the operations of the economy at large. And as it negotiates, as it starts to work and lose itself all at the same time, it is suddenly picking up speed, opening up new subjective territories we've never seen before, and contaminating all the other processes it engages.

When we speak into a cell phone, log on to the internet, or walk into a corporate brainstorming session, we enter into a kind of negotiation which puts our very being at stake. We discover a new acrobatics of presence, a metaphysical on/off-ness. We learn to make ourselves everywhere and nowhere at once, becoming adaptive, fluid, intuitive, risky, deterritorialised — everything an artist shares with every business in an information-based economy that works by constantly overcoming its own limits. These are our new skills and maybe the symptoms of a new psychosis — in any case, they are the things we use to navigate the permanent flow of money, information and bodies we call global capitalism. It is an adventure logged in real-time — in memos, emails, caller ID interfaces, but also on credit card receipts, by surveillance cameras, in corporate annual reports, databases and marketing studies. Scattered along a chain of communicating devices, this adventure discovers no outside, only different degrees of mobility or immobility on the endless inside. From now on, it is a question of tactical engagements with an occupied territory, as open as it is controlled, where our presence is determined as much by how we enter the processes which identify us as productive individuals as by our capacity to either overload or short-circuit these at the right moment. So we produce brand identities, testing the marketplace of ideas with provisional or virtual selves, replacing our face with a complex of interfaces or with a blank, company face. Thinking outside the box is also a question of our ability to abandon our position at a moment's notice.

Negotiation heightens our awareness of how circulation and control work together. Before we can be controlled, or control something else, we have to flow. We have to flow in order to pass through all the devices – linguistic as well as technological – that capital installs across its networks in order to manage its own chaos and make it profitable. Devices identify us, count us, track our movements, and gauge our productivity or lack of. They are like subway turn-styles — we pass through them at rush hour. This is how everything that moves and lives is put to work, every step of the way. Imagine an artist who locates her work precisely there where the global citizen is most put to work anyway. In the turnstile, in the training seminar, within the very processes that produce standardised, normative subjectivity, integrated go-getters, all the most advanced productivity-producing devices. Going for it right there.

Can we now start to imagine an art stripped bare, that casts off all the qualities – rebelliousness, outsider chic, critical distance, romantic genius, transgressive vulgarity etc – that have always allowed it to continue to show up as art? An art without qualities, seeking to integrate itself more effectively within the space-time of the global city it inhabits. This would be a supremely devious art that becomes in every way possible the thing that most wants to snatch its identity and put it to work, an art that makes itself happen on the verge of disappearance. But unlike the traditional conceptual practices it references, and whose tactics have already been absorbed by advertising and mass media, this upgraded version follows its immateriality all the way to the limit, to the point where it can no longer be distinguished from business, the old enemy it now doubles in turn. Business and culture: the uncanny experience of two processes disappearing into each other, exchanging places. And at the crossroads of this merger, the subject abandons fixed identity in the very act of self-actualisation.

When drowning, become a diver. Becoming-corporate in this way is to actively produce a zone where the processes of art and business lose their distinction. It is a zone of undecideability where what is business is always already the possibility of art and *vice versa*, where neither of these categories is ever completely present or absent (true or false), and where the negotiation between them is exhibited as such. And the game is to keep this space of negotiation – where lateral or transversal connections are provoked – shifting and intense, to make the work happen in this middle where things pick up speed. When there is no more escape from the marketplace, no more outside, subjectivity must continuously reinvent itself through negotiation and a proliferation of interfaces, emerging at the horizon of multiple, heterogeneous processes – economic, institutional, technological – where it can be exposed to the creative potentials that traverse them all. Always keeping an eye open to the unforeseeable, mutant territories this overlap

might engender. Negotiation itself is foregrounded as a creative zone —
creative precisely to the degree that whatever enters into it is always
undecideable and always at risk.

We enter the corporate world as a kind of giant, walk-in readymade. And to
preserve our mobility there, on the inside, we will need to invent a new,
rhythmic presence, an on/off music. Not only must we flow through the
devices, we must enter them with an agile undecideability. So it becomes a
game of taking and losing advantage. A tactical taking and losing of
positions and identities. By repeating or doubling the (normative, controlling)
processes that try to make us repeat ourselves, we make them repeat
differently. The difference is that we are no longer powerless before them.
We have made them follow us into this zone of negotiation where everything
that enters enters at its own risk.

What we see is this pin-striped body performing its own neutralisation by
Empire, as deep into the trap as it could go. Passing through the lobby of
a glass office tower, under broad daylight and security cameras, training
manual in hand, it couldn't be more exposed. It has taken on the words, the
clothes, the gestures. And this is how it constantly escapes: by showing up.
She passes, she gains access, she mingles, she negotiates in all of these ways,
an almost imperceptible art emerges, an art armed with the leading-edge of
capitalist schizophrenia.

Aha!

Nice idea.

Good point.

Seems like a winner!

That's a great idea. Thanks!

We're getting somewhere with this.

Hmm, looks like we could push that idea further.

Let's take that same concept and use it over here.

You know, this could be better than what we're currently doing!

Let's stay with that idea longer and see what mileage we can really get from it.

Positive Buzz
2001
Vinyl text placed on gallery walls by exhibition curator
Dimensions variable
Installation view at John Hansard Gallery

Statements prepared by the artist for 'creative thinking' workshop sessions, using the published advice of What?If! business consultants, London, who state that they have used this methodology for numerous corporate clients including airports, brewers and financial services companies. Statements can be placed together, separately or next to other works.

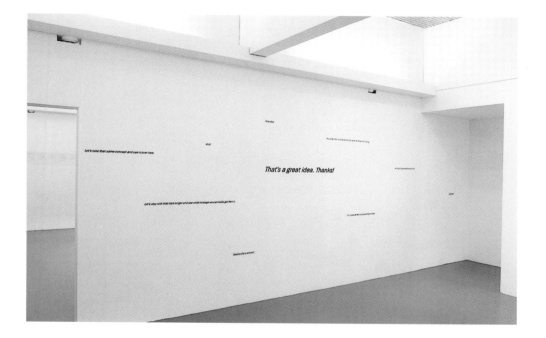

Gap Analysis

An annotated report derived from an evolving discussion between
Carey Young and Liam Gillick.

At issue are two distinct approaches to similar territory. One is
applied and apparently-integrated, involving processes of negotiation
and scepticism. The other is distanced and more abstracted,
focusing on the conditions that underscore the aesthetics of the
built world as they are affected by revised business practice.
The report here muddles the two, bringing statements together that
focus upon the working practice of Carey Young, in a form that is
the end-product of discussion with, and questions from, Liam Gillick.
The discussion has been published previously in two different forms.
The present structure is composed of question and answer
statements, with supplementary comments from both artists
included in parenthesis.

Answer/statement:

For nearly five years, I was working for an information technology and consulting multinational. When I joined, straight after finishing my postgraduate degree, I was interested in investigating mass-cultural visualisations of a technology-rich future. Although I felt uncomfortable with the idea of working within the corporate world for left-leaning political reasons, the potential of working in a progress-hungry technological environment was undeniably attractive from the perspective of deepening my own artistic research, as was the potential of setting up art projects involving my new colleagues, along the lines of the collaborative works I had done involving science-fiction writers and computer hackers.

I became attracted to the idea of dealing with corporate language and corporate behaviour at the point when I noticed that my own identity seemed to be in a process of transition. I had somehow, and quickly, become part of a corporate 'tribe'. *(Interesting paradox.)* I still remember where I was the first time I said 'we' and meant the entire corporation: a sort of personal 'merger' must have occurred. Considering Freud's essay 'The Uncanny', and taking inspiration from Hans Haacke, Marcel Broodthaers and Cindy Sherman's 'Untitled Film Stills', I began to make work investigating the process of concurrently gaining and losing my identity as both an artist and corporate insider, particularly because it seemed a fertile metaphor for the relationships between corporations and the individual. Through reading various anthropological texts on organisational cultures, I was able to reflect upon and distance myself from the processes of 'normative control', as they seemed to be happening to me, by which a corporation imbues new recruits with certain values and beliefs; particularly the notion that their own personal life-goals and the process of self-actualisation, in which a person achieves their own potential in life, can be realised, at least in part, within the corporation. People tend to joke about this as a kind of mind-control, like creating the 'Stepford Wives', but that's a myth — it's far more subtle. *(But that sounds exactly like the Stepford Wives.) (That is the point. I think part of the interest in this body of work is in its guessing-game around notions of autonomy and agency.)* It involves everything from specific training to the ways in which one becomes gradually oriented to an unfamiliar culture with its own norms, terminology etc. The purpose is to get maximum loyalty, pride and hence productivity from the employees, so in many senses the process is intended to make them feel great. The term 'symbiosis' seems rather more apt, in that there is a process of choice and allegiance happening on both sides.

My work often uses, challenges and exposes corporate training procedures and participative commercial systems as process-based readymades, to suggest these soft and kinetic boundaries, and the ease with which corporate messages are believed and internalised, whether at the level of becoming an employee, or within a wider social context. *(The process of taking on both politicised and depoliticised modes within a single work adds to this. It's like a game of cat and mouse, a complex position which asks the viewer to unravel the strands for themselves, and perhaps to find themselves equally implicated because they cannot completely condemn me for what I, or the work, might represent.) (Can they really do this in such a specific system?) (I believe so, but this is why I try to incorporate a sense of uncanniness within the work. The artistic identity of the work – often coming via the referencing of existing works by other artists – situates the viewer within an art context, but there is also a business identity which reveals itself, implying that the work exists concurrently in a parallel dimension of multinational business. To test this from another angle, I often try to show my work to interested businesspeople. If they have trouble recognising it as art because it is similar to something they themselves do or experience via their business career, then I know I am on to something, that there is a veracity to it. The 'site' of the work therefore can be seen to oscillate. A critic recently called one of my works as composed of and engendering 'data trails', which I thought was fairly apt.)*

Question/statement:
Recent readings of 'Walden 2', written by the behavioural scientist B.F. Skinner in 1948, affected some of the questioning. Although the book is appallingly-written and very clunky, it's interesting because it describes a utopian community living in the desert South West of America. It actually appears to describe a modern progressive corporate 'campus' environment. It seemed to pre-vision the idea of what the decision-making part of Microsoft or Nike might actually be like. A slightly dynamic situation which has fed on previous visions of what the future could be. A question emerged: how much do you think it is impossible to make the same value judgements people used to make in light of this kind of appropriation of progressive thinking? *(Double negative.)*

Answer/statement:
As corporate thinking, and business practice in general, has changed radically due to the fundamental shift to an information-based economy, so must the forms that its critics employ if they intend to be a constructive influence. *(It is arguable that they predicted and theorised it into existence, from McLuhan to Foucault.) (They may have predicted it, but it is only McLuhan that has been widely plundered by business 'gurus', mainly due to the fact that 'Wired' magazine held him up as some kind of patron saint at a time when the editors were advising the US government.)* This is probably also true for those intent on offering critical distance via cultural means. Business thinking is now voraciously nimble, especially at the level of advertising, where new subcultures are quickly understood both as a social demographic and as a set of trends. Transgression seems rarely able to remain transgressive for long. *(What about modes of refusal within business?) (They are simply valued as engines of progress, becoming the path of least resistance towards maximum profit.)* If a resistant ethos becomes hip, it will be marketed back to us as style: a sort of win-win proposition for

those consumers who want to associate themselves with bettering the state of the world, but who don't want to think too hard. Right/wrong or inside/outside binaries seem ever more outmoded. *(But they still affect left/right political loyalties.) (Yes, but do we still have the same notion of loyalty? It's like Debord says — the words for 'beer' or 'philosopher' stay the same, but the referent shifts, or is perhaps eroded.)* To me, it is a question of credibility: a singular stance does not seem credible any more. This is not to say moral slippage is acceptable, but I do not make work which moralises, and my reference to my own identity as a businessperson within my works is intended to say this most clearly, in that whatever commercial process or system I expose or make projects within, I still reveal myself at the same time to be included within that mechanism. It's not oppositional in a traditional sense.

Question/statement:
Clichéd construction of artistic persona leads to a situation where you are supposed to symbolise something better or worse, or more anti-social or more complex than the neo-liberal corporate structure. You are not supposed to be within the middle area yourself.

Answer/statement:
The artist as strategist is of course nothing new — Duchamp being probably the prime example. Perhaps it's the space of strategy that is at issue here. I tend to see it as somewhat of a lair. A median area (and for me the specific interest is with the innovation-hungry strategic operations of large corporations, and their effect on everyday life, particularly as a reworking of a Beuysian notion of social sculpture), could be seen as offering a new and rather overlooked 'edge' for precisely those reasons: a sort of avant-garde territory, with all the difficult cultural implications that it is business which now occupies an avant-garde position. It's rhizomatic — a space of 'becoming-corporate' as a metaphor for the spread of corporate influence. I am interested in revealing, inferring or creating chaotic structures within this flow — to employ Cildo Meireles' term, making 'insertions' into ideological circuits, rather than 'interventions'. This is more a process of distortion, slippage, or adding catalytic friction than actual disruption, because I have witnessed the mutual parasitism between corporations and the cultural sphere too often to think that the traditional notion of an artistic 'disruption', now, is anything other than a chimera, unless you are prepared to reinvent the category, as branding strategists tend to say.

Anthony Wilkinson Gallery
242 Cambridge Heath Road London E2 9DA
Tel: 020 8980 2662 Fax: 020 8980 0028
e mail: info@anthonywilkinsongallery.com
www.anthonywilkinsongallery.com

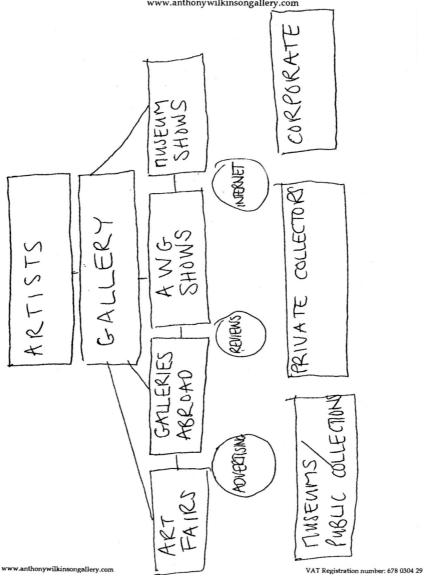

VAT Registration number: 678 0304 29

opposite
Incubator
2001
Distribution map
detail from 'Incubator: Project Report
(Anthony Wilkinson Gallery)'

above
Incubator
2001
Video still from documentation of
Visioning Workshop

below
Incubator
2001
Mixed media, Dimensions variable
Installation shows 'Incubator: Project
Report (Anthony Wilkinson Gallery)' as
installed at Anthony Wilkinson Gallery as
part of 'The Communications Department,'
curated by Alex Farquharson.

Participants:
- Anthony Wilkinson (Gallery Director)
- Amanda Knight-Adams (Gallery Director)
- Pól Ó Móráin (Xerox Venture Lab/Session Facilitator)

PM: If you compare art to say music, where the record company identifies an emerging artist and then puts a lot of resources behind them, the artist has a lifetime. Perhaps a two year period. If you take something like U2, the lifetime of the artist is quite long, and there's an ongoing revenue stream over quite a long period. But within that space you might have one release per year. Whereas with an artist whom you'd expect to last two years, you might push out the maximum number of music releases.

AW: And just capitalise...

PM: If you equate that back to the art market, how do you define the lifetime of an artist?

AW: You wouldn't really think of it like that.

PM: Why not?

AW: Well I never really think of it like that.

PM: What is your expectation in terms of when you start supporting an artist? In terms of how many pieces of work he or she should produce within a five year period?

AW: It's never really that clear cut. It depends on the artist and how quickly they work.

AK: It depends on what medium they use, painting, photography, video...

AW: It's not something we really discuss at the beginning.

PM: Have you ever considered different types of art than the number of outputs per artist, as against potential revenue?

AK: No, because it may not be the amount of work that's produced. An artist may produce one painting that may produce x revenue, but another may produce ten which may not bring in as much. We're not concerned with quantity.

AW: That's the thing about the art world, it's not really about quantity, a lot of it is to do with the rarity of it.

PM: But if you develop an artist, and you create demand or a profile or an expectation within the market, can you not then manipulate the market to sell more work of that artist, but at a higher price?

AW: Yes, but the thing is not to have too much work. That's not such a good thing.

PM: Because you're selling to the same audience? Or could you develop your audience and create more demand from the same artist?

AK: It's the idea of buying a unique piece of work, which is why somebody would spend so much on something they consider unique. If it was reproduced according to market trends then it wouldn't have the same effect.

PM: But if you take that piece of art and produce it in a hundred different colours then isn't that still unique?

AK: But that would be up to the artist. She would have her own reasons for
        producing that work of art in a hundred different colours, but that
        isn't a decision we could make.

PM: So you don't try to influence what the artists produce?

AW: Not really, no.

PM: And if you were, how would you go about it? For example, if you were
        able to demonstrate demand for a particular range or type of art, or
        artist.

AW: Artists make a body of work, and if it's being successful they may
        consider making that for a while. But they aren't just producing a
        product. It's other things as well. They wouldn't just continue making
        the same things for ever and ever just because it sold, because their
        careers wouldn't be developing.

AK: And the artists wouldn't respond to us well if we suggested that.

PM: Why not?

AK: Because we'd be making decisions about their work that they'd feel was
        theirs only to be made.

PM: But if you introduce the concept of art as a product, then if you can
        create a demand surely you can create the art on the other side to
        satisfy that demand? At least with some artists.

AW: Some artists make work that's in editions, like doing prints or
        something. A portfolio might have a much bigger run. With certain
        people, the nature of the work means they cannot make enough to
        satisfy... That's what creates the market. If there isn't enough work
        around, and they're in big demand, and one comes up at auction, then
        the price goes up because people can't get hold of the work.

PM: So the restriction of supply drives the price?

AW: Well, it's not mass-produced. If it takes an artist a month and a half
        to make a painting, there is just no way, however many people want to
        buy the painting, that they can make a hundred paintings in a year.

PM: If you take the equivalent in the corporate world, where you have
        joint ventures, you have companies who appear to be direct competitors
        in the marketplace jointly developing products and then getting
        individual revenues from that, or sharing revenues.

AW: Like, give us an example of what you mean.

PM: If you take the car market, where Ford motor company markets Ford
        cars, people have a preference for Ford's brand. But Ford also owns
        part of Mazda, and they also own other car companies, or part
        ownership, or jointly develop models and one company will sell it as
        their model in some countries, and Ford will sell it as theirs in
        other countries. So have you ever considered pushing artists in that
        sort of collaborative direction?

AW: Some gallery artists show with galleries abroad, so that sort of
        happens.

PM: But only on the gallery side.

AW: Say, one of our artists has galleries in America and two or three
        Europe, so they are all promoting the artist as well. That benefits
        the artist and also benefits us. Is that what you meant?

PM: My question was more on the artist's level.

AW: What you mean one artist working with another artist? Getting them to
        paint their pictures for them? (laughs)

PM: Well, if you take donkey carts, which were a form of transport, and
        you had individual craftsmen making donkey carts. Then someone
        invented the car, and you required a number of tradesmen to work
        together to produce a car. Then cars became mass produced.

AW: Well there are artists who have assistants, there are artists who
        don't make the work themselves. You can do that with certain things,
        but not really with a painting. Artists who do readymades, things
        which are produced by someone else, someone like Jeff Koons can get
        other people to make the work.

PM: So where is the value in his work, in terms of the buyer perspective?

AK: In the concept.

AW: The idea.

PM: So can you not replicate that in other forms of art?

AW: It depends on what the artist is trying to do, I think.

AK: No, a painting is a painting, it has to be done by the artist who is
        a painter.

PM: If you take look at this work here, could you potentially consider
        that that type of design could be marketed in other ways? In other
        words, if I develop a new way of printing things on paper, I have two
        options. I can satisfy the demand from anyone who knows about it, or I
        can go out and promote the fact I've developed this new way of doing
        X, Y or Z, and I can license it. So is there any aspect of what you
        perceive in selling art that could potentially be licensed?

AK: No, apart from a print or video that could be editioned. But it
        couldn't be editioned indefinitely. The supply would be restricted to
        how many was stated at first.

PM: Have you ever thought about going out and marketing artists' abilities
        rather than artists' work? So, for example, if you look at the
        advertising industry, where the whole emphasis is on creativity, where
        you create a concept ... I think Vauxhall cars is a good example. They
        had a 'crazy guy' for a while. They simply developed an advertising
        campaign based around the concept of this crazy guy and the
        relationship of that to their product.

AW: I don't think so, no.

PM: I don't mean in a like-for-like situation. But could you envisage
        situations where you can derive revenues from something other than
        just art as the product?

AW: You mean from the artist's personality?

PM: Or from their particular style of design?

AK: No, I don't think so. Maybe you could say it is taking away from what
        art actually is. It is unique within itself. If a certain design was
        used for something else...

AW: Art is used all the time in adverts, ideas are taken... well I suppose
        it works both ways...

AK: Well it's more of an influence, it's not using the artist in that
         sense.

PM: Well for example, I don't know which artist it was, but there was an
         artist who had simple pieces of paper with words on, and I think she
         photographed them on a bridge or something, I can't remember, but then
         that was taken up by some advertising companies. Have you ever thought
         about actually going out to advertising creatives...

AW: With our artists, saying "Put them in an ad" - no, I haven't...

PM: What I am trying to get at is maybe that doing those things doesn't
         produce important revenue streams, but it does create a brand or an
         image...

AW: Well I think we do try with the art press, and all that side of it,
         to get as much coverage as possible. On that side it does help a lot.
         If you can get work reproduced then it does make a difference.
         Artists' work that reproduces well always seems to do better than
         artists' work that doesn't.

PM: So if we go back to the idea of producing a brochure or fact sheet of
         what the unique selling propositions of art are, is there some aspect
         of what we've just been discussing that could be added to that list?

AK: So you mean in terms of using the artist in some other way? I can't
         see how we could do that.

PM: What I'm thinking about is trying to expand the segments we've been
         talking about. So, dealers, other galleries, individuals, corporates,
         government art collections and museums. From my perspective that is a
         very traditional structure that probably hasn't changed over a long
         time. And yet if you look at any other products out in the marketplace
         the routes to market, or the segments of the market are continuously
         expanding. So you create a product, and then you create demand for
         that product, and then you market it.

above
Video still from documentation
of exhibition preview

opposite
Publicity image for
My Megastore
2001
exhibition at Virgin Megastore
Oxford St, London

"… My voice will affect you, motivate you and empower you. The messages you hear will remain firmly embedded in your unconscious mind. It will be so natural to follow these instructions and benefit from them. Here and now, your unconscious mind can review and start integrating the formula for motivation power. It can reset your self-image to contain and reflect all your most powerful and successful qualities. And prepare to enhance them every day. Just let yourself receive this appreciation and assistance now. Remember feeling good and successful. See yourself now achieving, winning, enjoying life. See yourself in full colour: bright, clear and compelling. Get used to the real you, living your full potential. You can take all the hypnotic time you need to do this during this hypnotic trance. As this process continues, you'll drift further into trance. Every now and then, something catches your attention and then, once more, you drift off… deeper… comfortable. All the help and assistance you need comes from the unconscious mind. Right now, in trance, you can do what you need to do without straining, without worry. See your target now, focus on the achievements you're heading for. Make a clear, bright picture of the target you're going to achieve. See yourself in it, your family and friends, and see yourself enjoying the fruits of your success, your hard work, your happiness. Make that picture big, and bright, and compelling. Make sure every element of that picture is attractive to you in every aspect. And you know this is your future, and already you're heading towards it. Visualise your target in full colour. Bigger, brighter, bolder, brilliant and beautiful. Feel how good it feels to see this, and know this is your future. And let those feelings of accomplishment and wealth encode themselves into your neurology. Into every cell, every atom and molecule of your entire being. Whenever your mind is alert, focus on your target. Make that picture big and bright and bold, and bring it closer, and make the sounds louder. And feel those good feelings that are a part of your target. You know it is absolutely fine to succeed after several attempts. There is never any reason to be downhearted. In Hawaii, there's a tradition that a worried person would make a picture of all the things that worried them, and put them in a canoe. Then they would watch the canoe sail off out to sea, and watch it until it sailed right over the horizon. Over the horizon and out of their life. If you have any unnecessary worries, you can put them in a canoe right now, and watch them sail off out of your life. As you free your conscious mind to concentrate on success, you build up the energy to take action. Every day you'll do something to move towards your target. Every day you'll take action, and your unconscious mind will remind you you have the energy you need ready and waiting. You just start to work and the energy will become available. You become more and more responsive to your situations and the people you work with. Each day, you'll understand more and respond more to the forces and people around you. You'll become more and more flexible and adaptable, so that you can continue to work towards your target, whatever happens around you. Every day your tenacity will increase. You can keep going, persevering, achieving. Working and pressing on, so that every day you achieve something. Every day you move towards your target, and your unconscious will reinforce your motivation. Your faith in yourself grows and grows. You can have the unshakable confidence that allows you to be as flexible as you need. Know that you will achieve your target. Enjoy this sense of security. Say "Yes" to life, and feel the power of your motivation. Throughout this trance, your unconscious mind can run over and over the formula of motivation power, embedding it deeper and deeper into the patterns of your thinking, so it becomes second nature to follow the pattern. It becomes entirely natural and ordinary for you to be a highly motivated achiever. As your mind works in trance, you can take your time to relax…"

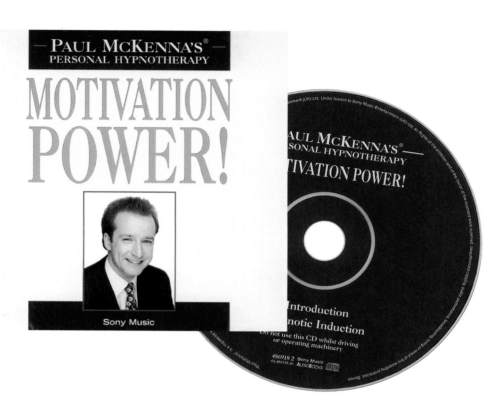

Personalisation
2001
Artist's playlist selected from Virgin's stock,
played on in-store radio station by exhibition
curator during exhibition preview
'Motivation Power!' text ©Paul McKenna, Hugh Willbourn 1992
with thanks to Sony Music

Cocooning
2001
CD, audio equipment
'Sleep Like a Log' ,Paul McKenna personal hypnotherapy taken
from Virgin's stock and placed on to in-store 'listening post'
Installation view

Workflow
2001
Video, 7 mins 30 seconds; colour
Installation view

Video, showing close-up of Virgin Megastore product-wrapping conveyor belt, was synchronised across all 16 in-store video monitors and interrupted the official music video playlist at random intervals during the exhibition.

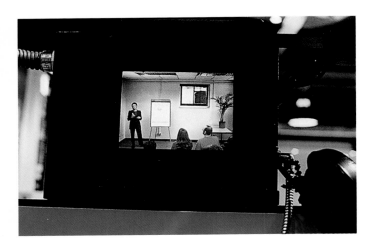

Buy–in
2001
Installation view at Virgin Megastore
Video, 26 minutes
colour, sound

Video documentation of performance by Carey Young to Virgin
Megastore staff, in which she explains the works in the
forthcoming show, stressing that their participation is essential
to the audience's understanding of the works in the store.

Always Smile at the Customer
2001
Electronic text on shop tills, Virgin Megastore
customer training manual
Image from video documentation

Sentence derived from Virgin Megastore staff training manual
and placed on to all in-store LCD till displays, facing the
customers, for the duration of the show.

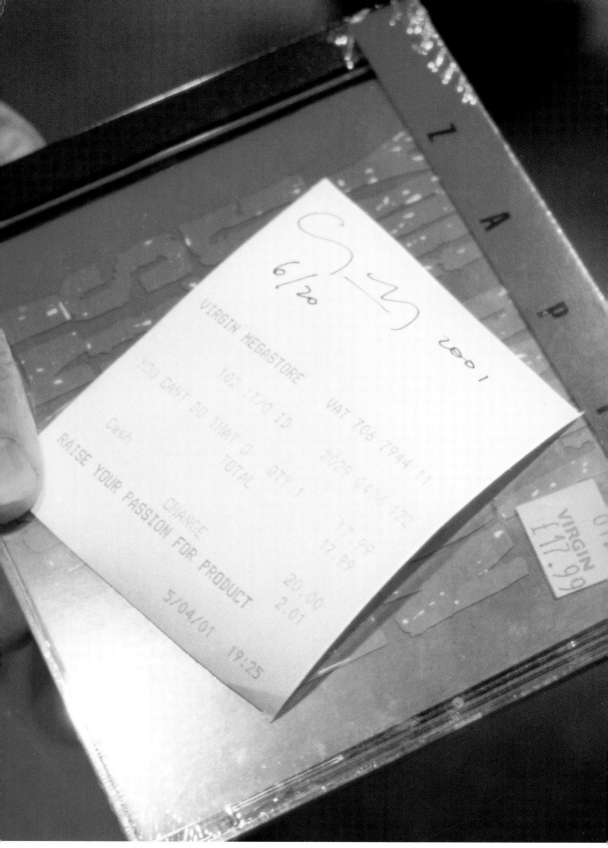

Raise Your Passion for Product
2001
Till receipts, Virgin Megastore customer training manual
Dimensions variable, edition upwards of 300,000

Sentence derived from Virgin Megastore staff training manual and reproduced on to all the store's till receipts for the duration of the show. During the exhibition preview, during which the store remained open for business and crowded with customers, the artist was available to sign a limited edition of 20, which necessitated the initial purchase of a product from the store.

Gap Fillers
2001
Whiteboard taken from call centre

Gift Economy
2001
Edition of 1000 white erasers produced for the exhibition 'Nothing'.
The exhibition logo was printed on the surface of each eraser.
The whole edition was available at the exit of the exhibition, as in
the manner of a trade fair.

above
Nothing Ventured
2000
Call centre, direct-dial telephone connection, telephone, desk,
chair, cassette recorder and tapes, ink on paper
Dimensions variable
Installation view, 'Nothing Ventured', fig-1, London

opposite
Nothing Ventured
Information pack containing reviews and CV, sent to callers on
request.

Date of call: 23 May 2000
                  Call 26 (excerpt)

Call Centre: Good afternoon, Carey Young, Nothing Ventured. Are you a member of the press, a prospective customer, or is this a general enquiry?

Caller: General enquiry.

Call Centre: OK, I can offer you a range of information. Would you like biographical information, previous exhibitions, themes and influences or reviews and review quotes?

Caller: Oh, I dunno. Review quotes?

Call Centre: Can I take your name please sir?

Caller: XXXXX.

Call Centre: OK. Carey Young's work has been reviewed in Art Monthly, the Guardian and Mute. A quote from Mute, "Young's work retains a ludic approach that should not be written off as co-opted."

Caller: OK.

Call Centre: Would you like any other information?

Caller: No, that's all thanks.

Call Centre: Right, thank you for calling. Bye.

Date of call: 24 May 2000
                  Call 31 (excerpt)

Call Centre: Hello, Carey Young, Nothing Ventured. Are you a member of the press, a prospective customer, or is this just a general enquiry?

Caller: General enquiry.

Call Centre: OK Sir. Can I just take your name please?

Caller: It's XXXXXX, Mr. XXXXXX.

Call Centre: OK, Mr. XXXXXX, I can offer you a range of information, would you like to know biographical information about Carey Young, her education, list of her previous exhibitions, her artistic themes and influences, or sales information?

Caller: Sales information.

Call Centre: Information on her photographic works are available in the information pack, which I can send out to you.

Caller: Oh right. I've got a phone here.

Call Centre: Oh, you are ringing from the phone in the gallery? You've come through to an information line about Carey Young's work.

Caller: Can I buy the phone?

Call Centre: The phone? Can I just ask you to hold the line please…

```
Date of call:      25th May 2000
                   Call 36 (excerpt)

Call center:       ... Her artistic themes are art and commerce, especially the
                   relationship between the art and business worlds. The readymade,
                   this is taking one object, calling it art and placing it in a
                   different context, i.e. a gallery. Hence the phone.

Caller:            Right, right, right.

Call Centre:       OK. Her influences are mostly the artist Joseph Beuys and his notion
                   of social sculpture - that everyone can create art.

Caller:            Exactly. So, in this whole, erm, formula, is the audience part of
                   the...

Call Centre:       Yes, they're actually part of the exhibition. As am I.

Caller:            Right, right. So you change the meaning with each conversation,
                   right?

Call Centre:       That's right.

Caller:            Fantastic.
```

```
Date of call:      27th May 2000
                   Call 13 (excerpt)

Caller:            Could you give me some influences?

Call Centre:       Um, the artist Joseph Beuys and his notion of social sculpture -
                   that is everyone can create art - is quite central, basically.

Caller:            Do you think everybody can create art?

Call Centre:       Personally. I mean, I'm not actually speaking for Carey Young, but
                   myself obviously, I think it's like a lot of people can do, yeah, I
                   think its all about expression, and obviously what Joseph Beuys'
                   concept was, basically, was that social sculpture is all about
                   reflecting the social structure at the time.

Caller:            Yeah.

Call Centre:       Everyone can actually create art.

Caller:            Yeah, right. Is that something that you believe?

Call Centre:       Personally, myself?

Caller:            Yeah.

Call Centre:       Yes, I think it is. I think it is, but I think it requires a degree
                   of expression and a degree of guidance, personally.

Caller:            Fine, OK. Are there any other influences that Carey has?

Call Centre:       Um, any particular influences. Sorry, if you could hold the line for
                   me for one moment.

Caller:            Thanks.

(long pause)

Call Centre:       Basically, there are a number of other influences on Carey. Um,
                   different artists, as you would expect. A lot of the themes that
                   Carey likes to incorporate are art and commerce. Especially the
                   relationship between the art and business worlds, and kind of
                   breaking down the barrier between two things that are opposite,
                   which in the past have been divided.

Caller:            So, how is she managing to do that?
```

Call Centre:	Umm, well basically um, there's all sorts of projects. Basically information, things like the 1999 exhibition 'Everything You've Heard is Wrong', which was a video of the artist giving a presentation skills workshop at Speakers' Corner. Which is kind of again breaking down the barriers.
Caller:	But how did it do that?
Call Centre:	How did it do that?
Caller:	Yeah.
Call Centre:	Well , I mean I think, obviously..., I can't really say everything that was behind Carey's thinking in this situation. Perhaps a better way I can actually, Carey can communicate this to you is by, maybe to begin with I can have some information sent out to you?
Caller:	You could do. I just wanted to get some information on the phone rather than a pack. I just wondered how you thought she broke down the barriers between commerce and art. If you could just explain that over the phone?
Call Centre:	Right OK. Sure, I can understand what you're saying. Um, its a tough question. I think what it is that in there are certain things are held taboo to art and taboo to business. And what Carey sees that these things can be broken down through the medium of art, because it is something which is a universal thing, and she said everyone can be involved in it, can make art. Whereas with business it's always been a kind of almost an antithesis, it's been the opposite.
Caller:	But do you think not everybody can be involved in business?
Call Centre:	Um, I think its the nature of, I think personally, the nature of the society we live in, it's not always the case that people, depending on their background can always necessarily get involved in. Fortunately I think it is something that is changing and I think that, I would like to think that art is one of the ways in which people can become successful.
Caller:	Yeah.
Call Centre:	And art is a form of music, in the form of video, in the form of film, in the form of anything, really.
Caller:	Yeah, OK. Thanks a lot for your help.
Call Centre:	That's OK, would you like some information by post?
Caller:	No, I think I can probably get that directly.
Call Centre:	Oh, alright, well thanks very much for calling. Don't forget to sign the visitors book in the gallery. OK?
Caller:	Right, I will. Thanks a lot. Bye.

Date of call:	27th May 2000 Call 13 (excerpt)
Call Centre:	OK, I'm back with you. Her themes are art and commerce, especially the relationship between the art and the business worlds. She likes the readymade. That means taking one object, calling it art and placing it in a different context, i.e. a gallery, as with the phone in front of you. She's influenced by the artist Joseph Beuys and his notion of social sculpture - that is, that everyone can make art.
Caller:	Sorry?
Call Centre:	Social sculpture.
Caller:	Social sculpture, u-hmm.

Call Centre:	Which means that everyone can create art.
Caller:	U-hmm. Is this the event of the readymade.
Call Centre:	Yes, it is that everything can be a piece of art.
Caller:	Right.
Call Centre:	OK, umm.
Caller:	Probably as long as the artist decides it's one.
Call Centre:	*(laughs)*

Date of call:	27th May 2000 Call 55 (excerpt)
Call Centre:	OK, Sir, I can offer you a range of information. Would you like to know about biographical information, previous exhibitions, artistic themes and influences, past work, sales information or reviews and review quotes?
Caller:	Artistic themes.
Call Centre: (short pause)	OK. Let's have a look for you. I won't keep you a moment. Let's have a look, here we go. OK. Artistic themes and influences. Art and commerce, especially the relationship between the art and business world, and the readymade, i.e. taking one object, calling it art and placing it in a gallery context.
Caller:	Yes, yes. OK.
Call Centre:	And influences - the artist Joseph Beuys, and his notion of social sculpture, i.e. that everyone can create art.
Caller:	Right.
Call Centre:	Would you like some information sent to your home address sir?
Caller:	I'll have it sent to my gallery address.

Date of call:	27th April 2001 Call 88 (excerpt)
Call Centre:	Good afternoon. Carey Young, Nothing Ventured.
Caller:	Good afternoon.
Call Centre:	Good afternoon. I can offer you a range of information. Would you like to know about the biographical information, previous exhibitions, themes and influences, reviews and review quotes, or information about this work?
Caller:	Biographical and themes.
Call Centre:	OK, just one moment please. Hold the line. Thank you, and your name, Sir, is?
Caller:	XXXXX.
Call Centre:	Oh, that's your surname, XXXXX?
Caller:	Yeah.
Call Centre:	Thank you. And you're interested in, was it themes and influences?
Caller:	And biographical.

Call Centre:	And biographical.
Caller:	This is uncanny. It's just like being at work.
Call Centre:	Is it?
Caller:	Oh yeah.

Date of call:	27th April 2001 Call 095 (excerpt)
Call Centre:	Can I take your name?
Caller:	Yeah. XXXXX.
Call Centre:	XXXXX?
Caller:	Yeah.
Call Centre:	And what's your surname?
Caller:	XXXXX.
Call Centre:	Thanks. Bear with me one moment please XXXXX?
Caller:	Yeah.
(laughs)	
Caller:	This is definitely a piece of art.

Date of call:	2nd May 2001 Call 116 (excerpt)
Caller:	Do you believe it's right that a public art gallery is shamingly promoting the .. shamingly promoting Carey Young?
Call Centre:	Right. Seeing as you're paying my wages, yes.
Caller:	*(laughs)* But what would you say if you were just a normal member of the public?
Call Centre:	I wouldn't have a problem with it. You either ignore it or you don't.
Caller:	But it's like, wouldn't it just be the same as like letting McDonalds or Coca-Cola into our art gallery?
Call Centre:	No, not in the slightest. McDonalds are capitalist.
Caller:	But surely Carey Young's just trying to make money.
Call Centre:	Of course. Everyone's trying to make money. We have to make money to live, and I'm quite sure that artists don't make very much money. When they've got the opportunity they should grab it.
Caller:	But surely she's just doing this so more people will go to see her exhibitions so more people will .. so her stuff will go up in value.
Call Centre:	Of course.
Caller:	So surely this is a shameless promotion.
Call Centre:	Not in the slightest.
Caller:	So do you think our conversation is really a piece of art?
Call Centre:	I definitely do. You are a form of art my love. Bye-bye.

Date of call:	May 2 2001 Call 131
Call Centre:	Hello. You're through to Carey Young, Nothing Ventured.
Caller:	Hello.
Call Centre:	Hello again. Can you hear me?
Caller:	I can.
Call Centre:	Hi. Yes. You're through to Carey Young, Nothing Ventured.
Caller:	*(pause)* Yes, I'm carrying on now.
Call Centre:	Sorry. Are we at cross purposes? Sorry.
Caller:	I think we might be.

Date of call:	May 2 2001 Call 133 (excerpt)
Call Centre:	Hi. Sorry to put you on hold there, I do apologise. How can I help you, Sir?
Caller:	I can't find the ink on paper in this installation. I was wondering if you could tell me where it is.
Call Centre:	The ink on paper? Are you actually calling Carey Young, Nothing Ventured?
Caller:	Yes, yes. It says there's a telephone and I found that; a desk – found that; chair – found that; direct-dial telephone connection – found that; call centre – that's your end; tape recorder; cassette tapes; ink on paper. But I can't find the ink on paper.
Call Centre:	Ink on paper. I think you may have dialled a wrong number, so just bear with me please.
(music)	

Date of call:	May 3 2001 Call 147
Call Centre:	Good evening. Carey Young, Nothing Ventured.
Caller:	Hello.
Call Centre:	Hello.
Caller:	*(pause)*
Call Centre:	Hello. Carey Young, Nothing Ventured. How can I help you?
Caller:	I'm not sure at the moment. I'll have to think about that one if that's OK. Right, thanks.
(hangs-up)	

To begin to think
about how we are to be
Joseph Butler & Jeremy Millar

[This text is a transcript of a short presentation given by the authors during a seminar workshop on creativity and corporate thinking which took place in London during summer 2001.]

Thank you very much for your introduction, and for inviting us to participate in this workshop. The title of this session ['Creative Organisations'] will give you some indication as to what we shall talk about — how might creativity be best organised, and can an 'organisation' itself be creative. Although this is a new context for us – we seldom speak in such well-upholstered surroundings – we hope that some of the ideas we are about to present, however briefly, will prove as useful in your work as they have in ours, as you've just heard [in the introduction]. Perhaps 'work' is not the right word, however. Perhaps we need to think more widely, and consider other forms of activity. Only then might we begin to approach a greater understanding of what it means to be creative.

As Johan Huizinga states at the very beginning of his classic study, 'Homo Ludens', "play is older than culture, for culture, however inadequately defined, always presupposes human society, and animals have not waited for man to teach them their play." Now, for all its apparent simplicity, play is complex. We might think of it as taking part in some activity or other, or as free movement of a mechanism within certain limits. In fact, it is many more things than this, although it might be useful to consider these two senses of the word during that which follows. In many ways it is a commonplace to consider play, or games, within a business context — decision-making strategy as developed through the moves of a chess grandmaster, for example, or the extended corporate playing field of games theory. However, we would like to begin with another game altogether, a very important one.

'Das Glasperlenspiel', or 'The Glass Bead Game' as it is known in English, was written by the German-born poet and novelist Hermann Hesse between 1931 and 1943. In one sense, the book is a fantasy set in an undisclosed future and, like all fantasies, it describes its own present just as clearly, if not more so, than its imagined future. It is the story of one Joseph Knecht, but it is also the story of the Game itself, and of our relationship to knowledge and spiritual values. The Game itself is never clearly described — indeed during the 'General Introduction' to the Game at the beginning of the book it is stated that: "The only way to learn the rules of this Game of Games is to take the usual prescribed course, whch requires many years; and none of the initiates could ever possibly have any interest in making these rules easier to learn." Some information about the Game is provided, however. It seems to have emerged simultaneously in both England and Germany, and was used by small groups of musicians and musicologists to explore memory and ingenuity. Then, in the Musical Academy of Cologne, Bastian Perrot began to use glass beads – which he moved upon wires held in an abacus-like frame – to replace notes, numerals or other symbols, and the Glass Bead Game came into being. As the Game was further developed, and the glass beads were no longer used, a common language was agreed whereby experts from different disciplines (who had developed their own specialist versions of the Game) might begin to play with each other; and so a game might progress from a line in a Bach fugue, to a sentence from Leibniz, or the layout of a Chinese house, or whatever, each move made with the greatest meditation, and each leading to the emergence of a new level of thought. "The Glass Bead Game is thus a mode of playing with the total contents and values of our culture... All the insights, noble thoughts, and works of art that the human race has produced in the creative eras, all that subsequent periods of scholarly study have reduced to concepts and converted into intellectual property — on all this immense body of intellectual values the Glass Bead Game player plays like the organist on an organ."

It was the Glass Bead Game which enabled the society to rise from its own cultural debasement, the past Age of Feuilletonism as it is described — that is, our own age. It is described as an age of trivia and irrelevant opinion. Newspapers are filled with crossword puzzles, and articles which merely "link a well-known name with a subject of topical interest." There are essays, too, in which the life or work of a famous man or woman is taken as the basis of an exploration of an altogether different matter. 'Friedrich Nietzsche and Women's Fashions of 1870' was one such example given. Might 'Hermann Hesse's 'The Glass Bead Game' and Organisational Strategy' be another?

We are aware of a couple of attempted uses of 'The Glass Bead Game' as a model for organisational strategy or development. In the November 1993 issue of 'Fast Company', for example, Paul Saffo calls Hesse's novel "the most important management book for the 1990s." He continues: "It combines leader-as-servant, pragmatic mysticism, creative destruction – in other words, all the business issues of the decade." There has even been an attempt to use 'The Glass Bead Game' as a textbook for flat management, although this seems at odds with the novel's emphasis on hierarchies, however constructed; as Knecht's title, and the title of the American edition, 'Magister Ludi' – 'Master of the Game' – makes abundantly clear. Indeed, Hesse's novel is far too complex – and contrary – to be able to provide a template or a set of simple rules for corporate success. The pedagogic utopia that is Castalia, where the novel is set, provided by society for the intellectual elite to grow and flourish, is not to be found in the high-tech parks skimming the M25, and a culture such as ours, which values chance and celebrity above all else, is unlikely to establish and support an intellectual culture based upon studious asceticism. Indeed, if someone looks to 'The Glass Bead Game' for simple solutions then we can be sure that they are certainly not in a position to find them.

Is there *anything* that we can learn from 'The Glass Bead Game' then? Are we allowed to play?

"Picture the following hypothetical scenario. Assembled in one room, are executives from finance, human resources, legal, manufacturing, engineering, information systems and marketing. Each of them represents a highly specialized discipline with its own vocabulary, formulae and notations. As they play the 'game', they find that each person has a distinct vantage point and unique ideas to contribute from their own discipline. The game progresses as each player moves his or her bead in response to the movements of the other players. Suddenly, one player interjects that the ideas played thus far can be synthesized into a new strategy which embodies each of the ideas, yet transcends them. The players move on to a higher plateau of knowledge, delighted with the emergence of a new, competitive strategy which they all contributed to and which will make them successful in the years ahead."

That description of a 'Game' in progress is from Mitchell Waldrop's book, 'Complexity', which explores the ambitious interdisciplinary projects developed at the renowned Santa Fe Institute. In this place, researchers from many diverse fields – physics, biology, economics and psychology, for example – come together in order to learn from one another, drawing upon the specialisms of others in order to make advances in one's own. And so ideas about information sciences might emerge from an examination of quantum physics or, to use an example with which you will probably be familiar, work in non-equilibrium systems might be used to develop the notion of increasing returns for a corporation, an idea developed by W. Brian Arthur which has been central to the anti-trust hearings against Microsoft in America.

What we have in this scenario, then, is not simply collaboration, a rather loose working-together tied with hope, but rather something more fundamental, more committed, something which we might call interdependence, or inter-relatedness, or reciprocity. In such a development, various people, or groups, or functions are not simply involved with one another in some co-ordinated manner, but each is committed to the success of the others, to the success of the whole, as this automatically means success for them also. In creating a mutually beneficial reciprocity – and sustaining it – the elements within the system benefit to an extent which would be impossible through more selfish means. A successful corporation is based upon successful *co-operation*, and it is the challenge of the corporation to develop an environment in which the benefits of positive feedback, of the type highlighted by Arthur and others, can emerge and creativity can become 'locked-in'.

We might describe such a system in another way also — as a holarchy. 'Holarchy' is a word coined by Arthur Koestler in his 1967 book 'The Ghost in the Machine'; one of two connected words, actually, with 'holon' being the other. Put simply, 'holons' are wholes that function as parts; a 'holarchy' is a larger whole within which these 'holons' exist. Of course, the relationship between 'holon' and 'holarchy' is one of scale, rather than a fundamental difference of type, as a holon is itself a holarchy, while a holarchy is, in turn, a holon also. (We could then say that the relationship is fractal, one which endlessly repeats itself at different scales.) What such a system allows, then, is a degree of specialism, or autonomy, but one which supports, and is supported by, a mutual dependence. As might be found round a table of Nobel Prize-winners in Santa Fe, for example; each working for the other and themselves simultaneously. And the result, to borrow a phrase from the anthropologist Gregory Bateson, is 'systemic wisdom'.

It is interesting that the idea of holonomy – the whole somehow being contained in each of its parts – might actually be a universal property of nature. This is certainly the conclusion approached by a couple of theories, Geoffrey Chew's S-matrix theory — which might be stated, provocatively, as 'every particle consists of all other particles' and David Bohm's notion of 'implicate order', in which all of reality is enfolded in each of its parts. But this is perhaps not the time, and we are certainly not the people, to begin to extend these theories into the given area of discussion, and so we shall return to an area in which we feel more comfortable.

[Music from a CD slowly becomes audible. There is an insistent rhythm made up from choral voices, a soprano saxophone and other brass instruments piercing through in their own rolling movement.]

You will recall that the Glass Bead Game was developed initially through the study and playing of music, and indeed music has a privileged position within the book. There is one section, in particular, which caught our attention. During a meditation lesson with the Music Master, in which the Master plays some themes and fragments upon the piano, the young Joseph Knecht floats within a void created by the music, and is able to watch it striding along, inscribing lines which he can then follow. Later, after dinner and just before retiring for the night, the Master invites his student to draw what he had seen: "the music appeared to you as a figure. If you feel so minded, try to copy it down."

After a number of attempts, the circle and curved lines radiating from it seem to satisfy Knecht and he falls asleep, only to dream of the landscape he had seen on his journey to the Master's house curve and spin like the musical lines which he had just drawn. These shapes seemed familiar to us also, although they are not reproduced in the book. We soon realised that the shapes which floated, spinning, before our eyes as we read were those drawn by the American composer Terry Riley and reproduced in the booklet accompanying the CD of 'Olsen III', to which you are now listening. (Here is that booklet, with those images.) We can only guess whether Riley had read 'The Glass Bead Game' by 1967, when 'Olsen III' was composed and performed, although Hesse's reputation in America was certainly growing amongst the counter-culture to which Riley belonged.

Riley developed 'Olsen III' during a one-month residency in Stockholm in 1967. He decided to create a work with a structure based upon a series of short motives or sections which the musician can repeat as many times as he or she likes before moving onto the next. The piece is probably new to most of you, and some of you may find it difficult to listen to. Certainly it was new and difficult for the Swedish musicians who first rehearsed it, particularly as Riley refused to conduct and instead chose to play amongst them. The relationship he tried to establish was not one of dominance and subservience, but one in which everyone had an important and equal part to play, each leading, each following, each listening to each other and to everyone together. While listening to this recording of the premiere, one can hear the movements between the musicians, the struggles and strains as the piece begins to lose shape and is then pulled back, as it interacts with their own exhaustion and with that of the audience. In such a work, the music plays the musicians as much as the other way around, a situation in which the process and its participants become indistinguishable, interdependent, reciprocal.

And so it is not simply the voices of the choir, singing out the phrases which we have taken as our title today, that encourages us 'to begin to think about how we are to be', but the nature or, rather, the structure of the music; a structure which creates the music anew each time. We believe that this is something from which we can all learn, whether we are attempting to organise a group of people within a department or a group of ideas within a work of art. This is not to surrender the principle of organisation completely; the music you are listening to is still a piece by Terry Riley even if, ultimately, he cannot determine the exact nature of the performance. Rather, he has created a system from which might emerge not just solutions which might not have been foreseen by any one individual, but solutions which *could* not have been foreseen by any one individual. In common with all musical performances, although here to a greater extent than most, 'Olsen III' is a complex system of both negative and positive feedback loops, some bringing the music together, creating its rhythms, while others move it apart, developing new themes and dynamic structures. In the CD's liner notes, the piece is described as 'simply like life'. We might go even further and say that it is a *form* of life, a form of non-organic life, like the economy perhaps, a system which is self-generating and self-organising, a system which demonstrates one of the most important ideas of non-linear dynamics, that from simple elements emerges unimaginable complexity.

The clock says that our time on the stage must end here also, but we would just like to leave you with the following thought. Although we strongly believe that it is crucial to create strong, interdependent systems (or ecologies as we prefer to think of them), such systems are not in themselves guarantors of creativity, benefits or success. As Arthur has demonstrated, it is not always the optimal product, or system, which becomes locked-in and emerges dominant (sorry to remind you, but think of MS-DOS). To develop a creative dynamic system is not the end-goal, then, but an initial set of conditions which are necessary if a process of self-generating creativity is to emerge, and only then through a rigorous play of feedback, positive and negative. As Bateson once warned, "There is an ecology of bad ideas, just as there is an ecology of weeds," and even some Glass Bead Games were better than others. It just depends on how you play.

Joseph Butler is the editor of *Ludicity — The Journal of Studies in Cultural Play*. Jeremy Millar in an artist and curator based in Whitstable.

Carey Young

1970	born in Lusaka, Zambia
1988 – 89	Manchester Polytechnic
1989 – 92	BA (Hons), University of Brighton
1995 – 97	MA Photography, Royal College of Art, London
	UK/US National; lives and works in London

Solo Exhibitions

2001/2002
Business as Usual
John Hansard Gallery, Southampton
Angel Row, Nottingham
First Site, Colchester
(curated by Film and Video Umbrella)

My Megastore
site-specific works at Virgin
Megastore, London

2000
Nothing Ventured
fig-1, London

Selected Group Exhibitions

2002
The Passions of the Good Citizen
Apex Art, New York

Exchange and Transform
Kunstverein, Munich

FAIR, Royal College of Art, London

2001
Ausgeträumt (Without Dreams)
Secession, Vienna
(curated by Kathrin Rhomberg)

The Communications Department
Anthony Wilkinson Gallery, London
(curated by Alex Farquharson)

Tweener,
Norwich Gallery, Norwich

The Doughnut Concept
Britart.com Gallery, London
(curated by Mark Beasley)

Nothing
Northern Gallery of Contemporary
Art, Sunderland; Rooseum, Malmö;
CCA, Vilnius; Mead Gallery, Warwick
(curated by Ele Carpenter and
Graham Gussin)

Look Out
Pitshanger Manor, London
(curated by Peter Kennard)

2000
Media_City Seoul
Metropolitan Museum of Art, Seoul
Seoul Biennale 2000,
(curated by Jeremy Millar &
Barbara London)

Continuum001
Centre for Contemporary Art,
Glasgow
(curated by Rebecca Gordon
Nesbitt)

the.year.dot
Aspex Gallery, Portsmouth;
Watershed, Bristol & tour
(curated by Film and Video
Umbrella)

1999
*EXIT, Art & Cinema at the End of
the Century*
Chisenhale Gallery, London

CRASH!
Institute of Contemporary Arts,
London

MayDay
The Photographers' Gallery, London
(curated by Jeremy Millar)

1998
Atomic
(with James Acord & Mark Waller)
ArtLab, Imperial College of Science,
Technology & Medicine, London;
Yard Gallery, Nottingham; Trdnjava
Kluze, Slovenia
(curated and organised by
The Arts Catalyst)

Outsiders
Center for Photography at
Woodstock, New York

Shine
National Museum of Photography,
Film & Television, Bradford

1997
*Zones of Disturbance/Zonen der
Ver-Störung*,
Marieninstitut, Graz, as part of
Steirisher Herbst
(curated by Silvia Eiblmayr)

Only Wankers Weep
Project Space, The Tannery, London
(curated by John Timberlake)

Wired/Elements
(with Stephen Livingstone)
Zone Gallery, Newcastle

We Meet Beyond the Sea
Vernicos Centre for the Arts,
Athens

Artifice
The Architecture Foundation,
London
(curated by Duncan McCorquodale)

1996
The Near and Far
British Pavilion,
Milan Architecture Triennale

1995
Stream
(with Sophy Rickett & Rut Blees
Luxemburg)
plummet, London

Reviews & Interviews

2002

Kelsey, John, 'Carey Young: Business as Usual', *artext*, Spring 2002

Suchin, Peter, 'Carey Young', *Frieze*, January

Parker, Graham, 'Nothing', *contemporary*, January

Kimbell, Lucy, 'What Business are You in?', *AN Magazine*, January

'Wie träumen? Eine Ausstellung in der Wiener Secession', *Neue Züricher Zeitung*, January 14

2001

Tan, Eugene, 'Carey Young', *contemporary*, December

Wilson, Rob, 'The Communications Department', *Untitled*, Autumn/Winter

Drabble, Barny, 'Trading Places', *Flash Art*, November

Beech, Dave, 'The Communications Department', *Art Monthly*, September

Bishop, Claire, 'Global Action East End Style', *Evening Standard*, 31 July

Herbert, Martin, 'The Communications Department', *Time Out*, 15 - 21 July

Tan, Eugene, 'Nothing', *Art Review*, June

Faucon, Benoit, *Les Echos*, June 15

Searle, Adrian, 'Empty Promise', *The Guardian*, April 24

Dodson, Sean, 'Art with a Message', *The Guardian*, April 19

Whitehouse, Christine, 'Young at Art', *Time* magazine (European Web edition)

Newsome, Rachel, 'My Megastore', *Dazed and Confused*, April

Herbert, Martin, 'Look Out', *Time Out*, Feb 21

Gellatly, Andrew, *Frieze*, January

2000

Mehta, Nina, 'The Business of Art, Carey Young Profiled', *Art Monthly*, November

Cukier, Kenneth Neil, 'When the Value of Art Outweighs Life', *Red Herring*, December

Gillick, Liam, 'A 90% Politeness Trustability Factor', *Make*, Sept - Nov 2000

Napack, Jonathan, 'The Taipei and Seoul Biennals: Video Sensations', *The Art Newspaper*, September

Stallabrass, Julian, 'Art I Like', *Modern Painters*, Summer issue

Rugoff, Ralph, 'Project Space with a Whirlwind Schedule', *Financial Times*, May 20

Mehta, Nina, *Art Monthly*, April

Donald, Ann, *The Herald*, February 21

Mahoney, Elizabeth, *The Scotsman*, February 18

Seymour, Ben, 'Everything Must Go', *Mute*, issue 16

1999

Weale, Sally, 'System C.R.A.S.H.', *The Guardian*, 28 November

Dodson, Sean, 'Art Workers', *The Guardian*, 18 November

Newsome, Rachel, 'Who's Putting the Boot in to Posh and Becks?', *The Observer*, 17 November

Arnot, Chris, 'Sculpting with Nukes', *The Guardian*, 26 October

Miller, Mara, 'What is the Subject in Landscape Photography?', *Photography Quarterly*, issue 74

Smith, Caroline, 'Carey Young', *Creative Camera*, February – March

1998

van Mourik Broekman, Pauline, 'The Two Hacks', *Mute*, issue 9

Jenkins, Milly, 'Technology with a Human Face', *The Independent*, March 17

Williams, Val, 'Shine—a light', *British Journal of Photography*, March 15

1997

Smith, Caroline, 'Wired', *Creative Camera*, December 97 – January 98

Gilbert, Andrea, *Arti*, November

Jenkins, Milly, 'Cyberspace on Earth', *The Independent*, 12 August

Lovink, Geert, interview, *Radio 100*, (Amsterdam), 4 August

Napoli, Lisa, *The New York Times* (online edition)

Flint, James, 'Visions of Cyberspace', *Wired (UK edition)*, January

1996

Williams, Val, *Creative Camera*, February – March issue

van Mourik Broekman, Pauline, 'Stream – Contemporary Flaneuses Take on the City – Sex, Surveillance & Science Fiction', *Mute*, issue 4

Guha, Tania, *Time Out*, Xmas/New Year issue

Residencies & Awards

Research Fellowship, Henry Moore Institute, 2002

Year of the Artist residency, East England Arts, 2001

Artist in Residence, First Tuesday, 2000

New Media Projects award, Arts Council of England, 2000

Eastern Arts Board Development award, 1998

Live Art Travel & Research award, Arts Council of England, 1997

Publications

Gillick, Liam and Young, Carey in Mir, Aleksandra, 'Corporate Mentalities', Lukas & Sternberg/ Nifca, New York, 2002

Rhomberg, Kathrin, 'Ausgeträumt', (exhibition catalogue), Secession, Vienna, 2002

Stallabrass, Julian, 'Internet Art: The Online Clash of Culture and Commerce', Tate Gallery Publications, 2002

'FAIR', exhibition catalogue, Royal College of Art, London, 2002

Slyce, John, 'Nothing Ventured', in fig-1 retrospective catalogue, Spafax Publishing, 2001

Gussin, Graham, and Carpenter, Ele, 'Nothing', August Media and NGCA, London, 2001

Millar, Jeremy, 'Escape' in 'Media_City Seoul 2000', (exhibition catalogue), Seoul, 2000

Dexter, Emma, 'CRASH!' (exhibition catalogue), Institute of Contemporary Arts, London, 1999

Flint, James, 'The Bright Tunnels of Alchemy, The Dark Lights of Science', in 'Atomic', (exhibition catalogue) The Arts Catalyst, London, 1998

Walton, Roger (ed.), 'Cool Sites', Hearst Books International, London/New York, 1998

Eiblmayr, Silvia (ed.), 'Zones of Disturbance/Zonen der Ver-Störung', Graz, 1998

Carey Young, 'Artifice magazine & CD-Rom', no.2, 1995

Art and Life
commissioned by Film and
Video Umbrella

*Everything You've Heard Is
Wrong*
commissioned by The
Photographers' Gallery, London

I am a Revolutionary
and *Getting to Yes*
commissioned by Film and
Video Umbrella and John
Hansard Gallery, Southampton

Nothing Ventured
commissioned by fig-1, with
additional support from
Film and Video Umbrella

Social Sculpture, *Force
Majeure*, *Positive Buzz* and
Incubator were produced as
part of a Year of the Artist
residency supported by
East England Arts

Cocooning, *Personalisation*,
Buy-in, *Always Smile at the
Customer* and *Raise Your
Passion for Product* were
produced in association with
the Virgin Megastore, London

Gap Fillers and *Gift Economy*
were commissioned for the
exhibition 'Nothing' by Northern
Gallery of Contemporary Art,
Sunderland

Carey Young would like to thank:

Jananne Al-Ani
Vaughan Bell
Steven Bode
Bevis Bowden
Denis O'Brien
Cleo Broda
John Browning &
Adam Sodowick
Ros Carter
Alan Clark
David Cross
Anders Edström
Nina Ernst
Alex Farquharson
Anna Fielder
Stephen Foster
Mark Francis
Liam Gillick
Graham Gussin
Alastair Haines
Matthew Hawkins
Ann Jones
Garrick Jones
Mike Jones
Frances Kearney
John Kelsey
Paul Khera
Maria Lind
Piers Masterson
Jeremy Millar
Aleksandra Mir
Kate More
Effie Paleologou
Michael Pinsky
Judy Price
John Sangway
Crystal Schaffer
John Slyce
Caroline Smith
Christine Sullivan
Tenyen
Andrew Warren

Anthony Wilkinson & Amanda Knight-Adams
Mark Wilsher
Pete Woodhead
Ralph & Angela Young
Bettina von Zwehl

All the artists at Occupation Road Studios

Alisdair Chisholm, Managing Director of Marcus Bohn Associates, the Business Skills Training Company

D.A. Associates

Bloomberg

Xerox Research Research Centre, Europe particularly:
Allan Maclean
Kimberley Moravec
Pól ó'Mórain
James Pycock
Mauritius Seeger

All photographs by the artist apart from:

cover. Untitled, from the series 'Correspondances,' C-Type 68x85 cm photographer: Frances Kearney
25. David Cross and Matthew Hawkins
26/27. Martin Figura
51. Effie Paleologou
54, 55 bottom right, 56, 59. David Pearson

Published by
Film and Video Umbrella
in association with
John Hansard Gallery
Edited by Steven Bode
Designed at PKMB
Production by Uwe Kraus
Printed in Italy

Published in an edition of 1,000

Publication supported by a Visual Arts Publishing award from the Arts Council of England, with additional support from the National Touring Programme of the Arts Council of England, John Hansard Gallery and East England Arts.

ISBN 0-9538634-6-8
© 2002 Film and Video Umbrella, the artist and the authors.

Film and Video Umbrella
52, Bermondsey Street
London SE1 3UD
Tel. 020 7407 7755
Fax. 020 7407 7766
Email. info@fvu.co.uk
www.fvumbrella.com